nd
ll

sbury, King's Cross
Iolborn

The East End
and Beyond

The City

he South Bank

uth of the River

THE
LONDON
COLLECTION

Rob Hinchcliffe, Mike Atherton, Matt Plaskitt,
William Wiles and Kenneth Yau

THINK
BOOKS

A Think Book

First published in Great Britain in 2006 by Think Publishing
The Pall Mall Deposit
124-128 Barlby Road, London W10 6BL
www.think-books.co.uk

Distributed in the UK and Ireland by Macmillan Distribution Ltd.
Brunel Road, Houndmills, Basingstoke RG21 6XS

Distributed in the United States and Canada by Sterling Publishing Co., Inc.
387 Park Avenue South
New York, NY 10016-8810

Authors: Rob Hinchcliffe, Mike Atherton, Matt Plaskitt, William Wiles and Kenneth Yau
Collection team: James Collins, Rica Dearman, Emma Jones, Marion Moisy,
Mark Searle and Rob Turner

ISBN-10: 1-84525-019-2
ISBN-13: 978-1-84525-019-5

Printed in China by Compass Press

The publishers and authors have made every effort to ensure the accuracy and
currency of the information in *The London Collection*. Similarly, every effort has
been made to contact copyright holders. We apologise for any unintentional errors
or omissions. The publisher and authors disclaim any liability, loss, injury or damage
incurred as a consequence, directly or indirectly, of the use and application of the
contents of this book.

London image copyright UK Perspectives

"Off to London, no doubt. Go to London! I guarantee you'll either be mugged or not appreciated. Catch the train to London, stopping at Rejection, Disappointment, Backstabbing Central and Shattered Dreams Parkway."

Alan Partridge, *I'm Alan Partridge* (1997)

INTRODUCTION

If you look out of the window to the left you'll see the Palace of Westminster while to your right...YAWN. Been there, done that, right? Pick up any guide book on London and you'll also find the same old same old. A few of them will even have no shame in dusting off that old Johnson chestnut, 'When a man is tired of London...'. Well this book is for people who are tired of 'that' London – the one that we all already know inside and out.

Of course, so many words have been written about our great city that it's hard to find an original voice. So we wondered what might happen if you took all those old clichés and, dare we say it, Hackneyed stories, and mixed them all up in a big cauldron of nonsense and whimsy. Hey presto, *The London Collection*: a rollicking open-top bus tour full of jellied-eel-crazed Beefeaters crashing through the Chelsea flower show.

This isn't a book for people who want to find the shortest route between Leicester Square and Oxford Street. We'd tell you, but we'd be lying. You will find no information about cheap places to eat in Richmond, unless you want to be told how to throttle a swan. We've gone out of our way to pull together some aspects of the London that we love and when we were in danger of drifting back to those traditional facts and figures we... erm... made some stuff up. Oddly enough though, it's the outlandish things such as the graffiti inside the House of Commons that turn out to be true.

Think you know London? Do you know which London bookstore sued the Pope? What Plato has to say about the Circle line? Where to catch the Green Wave? Why you're entombed the moment you step into a London phone box? Where the plaque for 'man about town' Topham Beauclerk is? We even have facts about Wombles that will chill you to the bone.

Sure, there have been other books about London. But we can say with confidence that none of them have the same ISBN code as this one. Several are better, but probably cost more and contain longer words. But if you're curious about a Top Trumps face-off between Golders Green Crem and Highgate cemetery, then please read on...

Mike Atherton, author

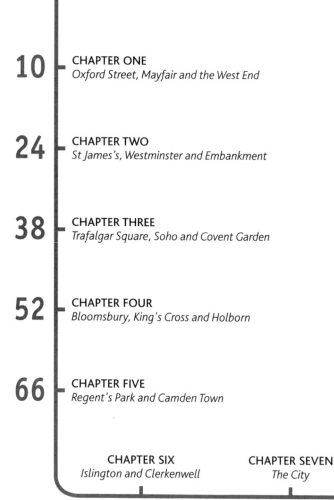

CONTENTS

OXFORD STREET
MAYFAIR AND
THE WEST END

OXFORD STREET MAYFAIR AND THE WEST END

NOW WHERE DID I LEAVE MY PHONE?

Londoners and visitors to London are the best in the world at forgetting to take their expensive gadgets with them when clambering out of taxis. According to a 2005 survey conducted by *TAXI*, the magazine for the Licensed Taxi Drivers Association, more than 60,000 mobile phones, almost 6,000 PDAs and a tad under 5,000 laptops are left in London cabs every six months, and subsequently end up in Transport for London's lost property 'graveyard', based near Baker Street.

It may simply be the shock of the fare from Waterloo to home that leaves passengers so bewildered that they simply forget so much gear. Or perhaps all this electronic flotsam acts as some pagan-like offering to the all-powerful black-cab gods who look favourably on the frantically waving pedestrians on rainy Friday nights.

But while Londoners forget more than double the number of laptops than other city-dwellers, they manage to mislay lots of other stuff, too. Other abandoned items have included a harp, a throne, £100,000 worth of diamonds, 37 milk bottles, a dog, a hamster, a suitcase from the fraud squad... and a baby.

'Are you a sinner or are you a winner?'

Philip Howard is one of London's most recognisable personalities, and yet you won't find him in any guidebook. As W1's self-styled 'manic street preacher' Phil can be found, come rain or shine, pounding the pavement of his Oxford Circus patch preaching the word of the Lord in his own inimitable style.

Part of that style included the use of a megaphone (until he was banned from using it), and it has to be said that it's this little gimmick that has made Phil the minor celebrity he is today. Whether you were innocently perusing the window display of Ann Summers on Oxford Street or sipping a quick pint somewhere off Regent Street, chances were you could hear Phil's peculiar remonstrations way before you caught sight of his distinctive blond thatch. Maybe it's the Scouse accent that makes Phil's diatribes so memorable. More likely it's his use of rather contrived rhyming couplets – 'Are you a sinner or are you a winner?' being his favourite. Whichever, you really can't call yourself a proper Londoner until you've been dubbed a 'lost soul' by this most ardent member of the God fan club.

A little known fact about Mr Howard: he used to believe he was a werewolf and would ask the police to lock him up come the full moon.

> The only thing I have of value, is this [pulls out a necklace with a tooth on it]. Jimi Hendrix's tooth, there was a fight in a pub down Oxford Street, someone planked him, and I picked it up. I knew he was a genius even then.
>
> Stephen Rea as Tony Costello in *Still Crazy* (1998)

My husband went to London and all I got was this lousy surveillance device
(Unusual gifts for the family, available from the Spy Shop on South Audley Street)

- A portable audio transmitter disguised as a pocket calculator.
- A 'reliable and easy to use' bug detector.
- A video surveillance equipment disguised as a picture frame.
- A chemical attack pack including carbon filter respirator and a pair of air-tight goggles.
- A 'gentleman's necktie' that contains a high-quality, colour pinhole camera.
- An electro-magnetic rodent repellent (to deter spying rats?)

The Trocadero Centre

has its good points and its bad points. The good points include the mole-bashing game in the arcade (great for getting rid of any pent-up frustration), plus the fact that it hosts the brilliant Raindance Film Festival every year. And, though we're loathe to admit it, we still retain fond memories of the mid-1990s 'Alien War' attraction where out-of-work actors dressed in rubber costumes scared the bejesus out of us for just under seven quid a time.

As for the downside, well where do we start? The term 'tourist trap' could have been invented for the Troc. Make the mistake of stepping on the wrong escalator and you can end up in what seems to be an Escher painting full of screaming tweenies. Be warned, if this happens you might as well give up any hope of ever seeing your family again.

It's all a far cry from the building's origins in the 1890s, when J Lyons & Co erected the Baroque palace to house their famous restaurant where women were (gasp!) allowed to dine alone and which the *Penny Illustrated Paper* called 'the most brilliant new sight in London'.

In 2006, it was announced that the Troc's new owners were to turn the vacant upper floors into a swish hotel, and that the rest of the building would be modernised in order to 'create a brighter, more open and attractive environment for all'.

Good luck to them. As long as they keep the mole-bashing game we'll be happy.

IT'S A KIND OF TRAGIC

Of all the ways to go, drowning in beer has got to be up there with sexual overexertion and (literal) death by chocolate. And once upon a time, in Tottenham Court Road, drowning in beer is exactly what happened. To lots of people.

You're probably familiar with the oversized Freddie Mercury statue gurning from the entrance to the Dominion Theatre. Before it was given over to flamboyant rock operas, this spot was occupied by Meux's Horse Shoe Brewery. The brewery housed a great porter vat, which stood 22ft high and could hold the equivalent of over a million pints under pressure. So, you wouldn't want to spill it.

Unfortunately, in 1814, one of its metal hoops gave way, causing the contents to break free. The ensuing wave of ale swept headlong through the crowded 'rookeries' of St Giles with devastating effect. To cries of 'save me', eight people were killed by debris, drowning and fumes. And, through sheer drunkenness, another one bit the dust.

At this far remove, it's easy to be flippant about the tragedy. Still, who wants to live for ever?

> About six o'clock I went home, dressed, dined at the Café Royal, and turned into a music-hall. It was a silly show, all capering women and monkey-faced men, and I did not stay long. The night was fine and clear as I walked back to the flat I had hired near Portland Place... At Oxford Circus I looked up into the spring sky and I made a vow. I would give the Old Country another day to fit me into something; if nothing happened, I would take the next boat for the Cape.

John Buchan, *The Thirty-nine Steps* (1915)

SPRINGTIME FOR HITLER...
a selection of real-life West End flops

Maybe That's Your Problem – A comedy starring the young Elaine Paige. It managed to be a flop in more ways than one as the story centred around premature ejaculation.

Behind the Iron Mask – A musical based on the Alexandre Dumas novel and starring former Three Degrees singer Sheila Ferguson. Closed two days after opening.

The Fields of Ambrosia – 'The Fields of Ambrosia, where everybody knows ya.' A musical about a travelling executioner, his electric chair and his love for his first female client... Did well in the States but suffered in London where it closed after 23 performances.

Umoja – A South African show at the Shaftesbury Theatre which was forced to close by Camden Council after local residents complained about the noise.

Murderous Instincts – Originally publicised as 'The Salsa Musical', this was scrapped when it was realised that none of the cast knew how to salsa. It cost a reported £2 million and closed after just over a week.

Oscar Wilde: The Musical – Written and directed by DJ Mike Reed, and with a script consisting entirely of rhyming couplets. We can't imagine why it closed after one night.

Money to Burn – Part thriller, part farce, part satire and including songs in the 'jazz pop' style. *The Daily Telegraph* called it 'jaw-droppingly dreadful' and it closed after two performances.

Well, now, then, let me see. I get up at about 7.30am, making and delivering sandwiches in the West End during the day before I come here about 6 o'clock and finish at midnight. After that, if I've got any energy left, I give my boyfriend a blowjob.

Gwyneth Paltrow as Helen in *Sliding Doors* (1998)

PAOLOZZI'S EDUARDO TCR MURALS

Tottenham Court Road tube station (TCR) is undoubtedly one of the most frustrating examples of urban planning in the entire capital. With its cramped ticket hall and disorientating layout, at times it's difficult not to believe that the station's designers weren't just trying to cause London's commuters to turn on each other in some apocalyptic, *Mad Max*-style brawl.

Unfortunately there's also a very good reason why you should take a trip to this most dismal of stations. Eduardo Paolozzi was a Scottish artist of Italian descent whose bizarre and brilliant work appears across many London locations, the most famous probably being the statue of Isaac Newton in the forecourt of the British Library.

TCR station is home to no less than 1,000 square metres of Paolozzi mosaic. Saxophones, bulls, chickens, the Hubble Space Telescope, strange mechanical devices: they all appear in this surreal and strangely endearing technicolour landscape.

And the most ironic thing? If TCR were to finally get the redesign it so badly needs it's very likely that much of Paolozzi's work would get completely destroyed. Even more reason to go see it now while you still can.

INVISIBLE MEN

It's often said that living in a big city like London can bring about a distinct sense of anonymity and even lead to feelings of invisibility. Nowhere is this more true than in among the jostling elbows and averted gazes of London's West End, so it's not surprising that the area has a distinct history of people disappearing into the ether.

The most successful instance (albeit a fictional one) is when HG Wells's eponymous Invisible Man spends the whole of a chapter bumbling around Oxford Street and the surrounding area, mainly because he hasn't quite got used to not being able to see his own feet.

Slightly less successful were the experiments of the infamous Satanist Aleister Crowley. Legend has it that on at least one occasion Crowley covered his body in scented oil, donned his 'invisibility cloak' and marched into the Café Royal convinced that no one could see what he was up to.

One version of the story has the Café's clientele studiously ignoring Crowley, as only the English can do, thereby convincing the mad magician of his abilities. Another version ends with a frustrated waiter confiscating the magic cloak only to find Crowley naked underneath. It's enough to put anyone off their cappuccino.

OXFORD ST
not just for shopping

Contrary to popular belief Oxford Street is not just one big retail-orientated hellhole. In fact, if you take the time to scratch away at that consumerist surface it is possible to find some real cultural nuggets tucked away in-between the cash registers and the BOGOFs.

The most famous of these hidden arty enclaves is the Wallace Collection. This extensive collection of *objets d'art* is housed in Hertford House, Manchester Square, just off the Marble Arch end of Oxford Street.

Containing works by Titian, Rubens, Reynolds, Van Dyck and Canaletto, this is also the home of Frans Hals' *Laughing Cavalier*. And there's even a rather nice garden out the back.

For something more contemporary, you need to go up past Oxford Circus and take a right on Poland Street to reach the Blink Gallery. This place deals mainly in contemporary photography aimed at Soho urbanites, so there's lots of pouting rock icons and sports stars.

And if contemporary snaps are your kind of thing you'll want to cross over to the other side of Oxford Street on to Eastcastle Street where you'll find the Getty Images Gallery. Here they regularly plunder one of the largest image archives in the world for their free exhibitions, which are always worth a look.

You'll probably be all cultured out by this point so your final stop should be to sample the distinctly lowbrow but brilliant delights of the Animation Art Gallery. Here the walls are covered with original drawings of everyone from Mickey Mouse to Homer Simpson, Thomas the Tank Engine to the Mr Men. Just don't take the kids!

Most impressive people
who've switched on the Regent Street Christmas lights

Sylvester Stallone (1993)
Sir Anthony Hopkins (1992)
Kylie Minogue (1989)
Joan Collins (1985)
Diana Princess of Wales (1981)

A WEST END MENAGERIE
(without resorting to pub names)

A Bathing Ape – Achingly hip Japanese clothes shop situated on Upper James Street.

Crazy Bear – Trendy bar and restaurant on Whitfield Street (has cowhide barstools to boot).

Mandarina Duck – the London branch of the Italian upmarket 'plastic bags' manufacturer can be found on Conduit Street.

Black Dog Music – Berwick Street's finest purveyors of that 'dance music' all the kids are into these days.

Tiger Tiger – Based on Haymarket, near Piccadilly Circus, this bar might have been cool once but is now seen as a bit of an 'upmarket meat market'.

Wolfe's restaurant – This old-school bar and grill on Great Queen's Street is famed for its burgers and was the first place in the UK to serve Kobe beef.

Octopus – to be found on Carnaby Street, this lot introduced London to the 'Barnaby', a pig-shaped bag with a curly tail, and we'll never forgive them.

Fish – A hairdresser's situated in an old, art-deco fishmongers building on D'Arblay Street. Famous for the indie-tastic 'Soho crop'.

The Hippodrome – oh, come on, it's close!

'Imagine if all this money was real...' Say the word 'Mayfair' to just about anyone in the developed world and you can pretty much guarantee they won't be envisaging the actual area. Instead they'll be thinking about the enticing dark blue square that lies at the end of the Monopoly board, just before you pass 'Go' and collect your £200.

We all know that Mayfair is the priciest of all the Monopoly properties, but it is also the only square that doesn't represent a real-life street. (OK, so you won't find The Angel Islington in your A-Z, but Islington High Street does run past Angel tube station.) There is a 'Mayfair Place' but it's so small that we can't really take it seriously.

In the summer of 2005, a 'Here and Now' edition of the game was released that dared to oust most of the traditional destinations and replaced Park Lane and Mayfair with Canary Wharf and The City. The prices went up as well: people who were used to paying £400 for Mayfair suddenly found themselves laying out a tidy £4 million for The City. And if Monopoly were real life? Well, then Madonna would undoubtedly be winning. She currently owns three separate properties on one street in Mayfair.

HERE COMES THE RAIN AGAIN

When it starts raining you'll find many Londoners simply hold a newspaper over their heads and frown a bit. We're used to it and, indeed, some would argue that the *Evening Standard* is good for little else. However, when the cats and dogs really start falling you'll find the more refined inhabitants of the capital gravitating towards James Smith & Sons, the oldest and largest umbrella shop in Europe.

It's situated on New Oxford Street just a couple of minutes away from the junction with Tottenham Court Road, and there's really no danger of missing the place. The building has remained unchanged for the past 100 years, and the shop's frontage is a perfect reminder that the Victorians really knew what they were doing when it came to 'retail design'.

Although a great deal of Smith & Sons' business comes from passing trade (especially when there's a few grey clouds about) much of it also comes from abroad, with a steady stream of Americans arriving to buy quality canes or walking sticks that are apparently difficult to find Stateside. Tribal chiefs of South Africa also prefer to use Smith & Sons when it comes to sourcing their ceremonial umbrellas and maces.

Although the shop stocks a good selection of common-or-garden umbrellas starting at around the £10 mark, one of their biggest sellers is a rather chilling version of the standard black umbrella, topped with a silver skull. A big hit with surgeons and Goths alike, it will set you back nearly £300.

And it's not all umbrellas and canes. There's an impressive array of shooting sticks, some very fine hip flasks and even a silver backscratcher with a price tag of £165.

Don't be fooled by the sign outside, which promises 'dagger canes and sword sticks' though. That's just there because the shop's signage is listed and can't be removed. It became illegal to carry a lethal weapon disguised as a walking stick around the 1980s.

> **Life, how I have dreaded you... oh, human beings, how I have hated you! How you have nudged, how you have interrupted, how hideous you have looked in Oxford Street, how squalid sitting opposite each other staring in the Tube! Now as I climb this mountain, from the top of which I shall see Africa, my mind is printed with brown-paper parcels and your faces. I have been stained by you and corrupted.**
>
> Virginia Woolf, *The Waves*, (1931)

LEAST IMPRESSIVE PEOPLE
who've switched on the Regent Street Christmas lights

Busted and 'The Incredibles' (2004)

Leslie Joseph, Rolf Harris, Britt Ekland and Lionel Blair (1995)

David Ginola accompanied by girl band Loose Chippin's (who?) (1999)

John Major (1996)

NB: At the time of going to press the official Regent Street website states that 1980's entrusted celeb was 'David Essex, of *Only Fools and Horses* fame'. A statement which could only be funnier if it were actually true.

I USED TO BE A WEREWOLF BUT I'M ALRIGHT NOWOOOOH

In the classic 1980s horror flick *An American Werewolf in London* there is a particularly gory scene that takes place inside the confines of Tottenham Court Road tube station. Obviously next time you're there you'll want to re-create that scene so here's a few pointers to help you get things just right.

Enlist a friend. One of you will play the wolf while the other takes the role of the hapless commuter... or 'supper'.

A particularly hirsute friend would be great, otherwise one of you will have to cover yourself in double-sided sticky tape and roll around on the floor of your local hairdresser's to create the desired effect.

Make your way to the Northern line branch platform. In the film the wolf conceals himself in the tunnel; we advise against this as you'll end up being arrested (plus, there's mice in there, eww). Just crouch behind one of the chocolate machines instead.

In the movie the victim gets off the tube to find he's the only person on the platform. Warning: if you wait for this situation to arise you are going to be waiting one hell of a long time. Just get on with it, the people who pass through TCR every day have seen much weirder things than you prancing around in hairy sticky tape.

Now chase each other round the station growling and screaming until you get disorientated and scared (not difficult at TCR).

Eat your friend on the up escalator but be sure to stay on the right-hand side so as not to block the way.

WINE FRENZY IN THE WEST END In 1997, Stephen Twigg was on top of the world. He'd just unseated the unbearably smug Michael Portillo, MP, from the previously safe Tory stronghold of Enfield Southgate and been cheered to the rafters for his achievements.

However, just a few short years later all was not well. In the 2005 election, Twiggy lost his seat to Conservative Party candidate, David Burrowes, by a margin of 1,747 votes in another shock result.

Then, in December the same year, the former schools minister became the first casualty of the Christmas party season. Following a bit of a knees-up at a restaurant on Orchard Street, Twigg was clocked by local constabulary tripping up as he exited what *The Times* newspaper later described as a 'wine frenzy'. Twigg was in such a state that police had to take him to Marylebone police station and present him with a £50 fixed penalty notice for being 'drunk and incapable in a public place'.

And at what ungodly hour did this debauched display of unbridled hedonism take place? Quarter past seven in the evening.

FLUSHED WITH PRIDE

Loos are important to Londoners. OK, so we don't talk about them over dinner or anything, but lavatorial discussions take place all the time in the capital.

In May of 2006, for example, some emergency refurbishments had to be carried out at Brixton prison when Muslim inmates realised that they were facing Mecca while using the toilet. At around the same time Mayor Ken Livingstone boasted to the press that, for the sake of the environment, for the past 15 months no one in his household has flushed the john after urinating!

However, it's public lavs that cause the most consternation. Recently a self-proclaimed 'panel of expert witnesses' met at the London Assembly to discuss the fact that the city had lost 300 public conveniences in six years. Despite the fact that Urilifts (urinals that rise out of the pavement at peak peeing times) had been installed in the West End at the turn of the millennium, the problem of rogue-relieving had become the most complained-about form of antisocial behaviour in the city.

Fortunately for anyone caught short near the Marylebone Road, the area does offer something a little above the 'bog standard'. Situated close to Baker Street tube in the vicinity of Madame Tussaud's, these public loos, with their piped classical music and painted tiles depicting the area's history, are definitely the VIPs of WCs. And you don't even have to pay to use them.

THE GREEN WAVE

Unless you're a motorcycle courier or heavily into town planning, you've probably never heard of the 'green wave' phenomena.

Dreamt up by traffic management geeks, the green wave is an attempt to synchronise the recommended driving speed along a certain section of road to the system of traffic lights on that same route. This would create a magical nirvana of 'continuous traffic flow' where everyone is happy and joyous and no one shouts or makes obscene hand gestures.

London has its very own green wave situated on the Marylebone Road between King's Cross and the Westway. This permanently log-jammed couple of miles can, it has been rumoured, be navigated without stopping if the conditions are just right.

Unsurprisingly, those conditions include making the journey in the dead of night and maintaining a constant, steady speed.

Motorists who have surfed this legendary wave (and they're mostly black-cab drivers) have spoken of a truly metaphysical experience that transcends all other joyous driving moments, such as outfoxing traffic wardens or hitting an empty stretch of the M25 just as Queen's 'Don't Stop Me Now' comes on the radio.

"Get out of my way!"

If you were to walk down a deserted Oxford Street at a steady pace of 4mph, it should take just 19 minutes to walk the 1.25 miles. However, until such time that an apocalyptic plague wipes out the rest of humanity you're going to have to put up with getting nowhere fast. People are working on a solution, however. In 2005, Mayor Ken Livingstone proposed re-routing all the buses to ease congestion. Just a year earlier the Lib-Dem rival for the Mayoral office, Simon Hughes, had put forward a slightly more drastic solution: pedestrianisation and the installation of a tram system. But he failed to get himself elected, so that was that.

A slightly more futuristic plan was proposed in 2005 by Westminster councillor Ian Wilder: monorails. 'Monorails work,' he told the press before getting a little carried away, declaring: 'We can morph the stations into the side of buildings,' to the sound of stifled giggles.

Perhaps the most fanciful idea came at the turn of the millennium from a campaign group fed up with increasing incidents of 'pavement rage'. They demanded the installation of a pedestrian fast lane, to be patrolled by marshals armed with cattle prods to ensure people in the special zone didn't fall below 3mph. OK, so we made the bit about cattle prods up. But the rest is true, honest.

ST JAMES'S
WESTMINSTER
AND EMBANKMENT

ST JAMES'S
WESTMINSTER
AND EMBANKMENT

THE HIDDEN WATERGATE

The River Thames lost a few inches around the waist 140 years ago – 4,000 inches on the north bank alone. Joseph Bazalgette's remarkable Embankments were wot dunnit, narrowing the river and reclaiming many acres of land, as well as carrying a broad roadway, a sewer and what is now the District line. A tangible reminder of this vast accomplishment is the old watergate in Victoria Embankment Gardens – a seventeenth-century river portal has been left high and dry by the retreating river. Rusticated and ornamented almost to the point of hilarity, the gateway once served river traffic to the long-vanished York House. Now it's not even visible from the river, tucked away in a leafy corner of the park.

There are, however, other subtle reminders of the the Thames's vanished shore. The Strand once ran along the river bank, and takes its name from the beach it overlooked. And at Somerset House, which once faced directly onto the river, there is a preserved archway for the entrance of barges into the palace. It's now on display under glass at the Embankment entrance.

PAY ATTENTION NOW

- Embankment tube station used to be called Charing Cross and the station just below it was called Embankment. Charing Cross used to be called Trafalgar Square.
- Charing Cross (Embankment) and Charing Cross (Strand) were then added, just to wind tourists up.
- Charing Cross (Embankment) became Charing Cross; Charing Cross (Strand) became Strand.
- So that left you with Charing Cross, Strand, Trafalgar Square and Embankment. Phew.

- Except there already was a Strand so they renamed that one Aldwych.
- Then Strand was closed because of the Jubilee line.
- Which was called the Fleet line.
- When the Jubilee line opened the mess was divided between what are now Embankment and Charing Cross.
- But legend has it that on a winter's night, under a full moon, the ghost of Strand and the spectral image of Trafalgar Square surface to look for more unsuspecting passengers...

LONDON'S ONLY PISSOIR

Horseferry Road, just south of Westminster, is best known for the Channel 4 headquarters, designed in the hi-tech style by Richard Rogers and built in the early 1990s. It looks a little like a greenhouse crossed with an oil rig.

A little further along the road, however, is a humbler but no less curious structure: London's only pissoir. Pissoirs are (very) public conveniences formerly popular in France. It is – and there is no delicate way of putting this – an open-air booth for peeing in. So, gents, worth bearing in mind if you find yourself caught short while on the way to Channel 4 to punch out Russell Brand.

Westminster council has, however, come close to rediscovering the pissoir as part of its efforts to stop drunken Londoners widdling against buildings. Soho Square is now graced by a sort of techno-pissoir. At a certain point of an evening – maybe when some dread algorithm in City Hall calculates that Soho's collective bladder is full – these shining steel columns rise silently from the pavement, a bit like that thing in the middle of the TARDIS control deck, for use by a thankful (male) public.

UNFINISHED BUS(H)INESS

There's an unfinished building on Aldwych, but you'll have to look hard to find it because it has been 'under construction' for more than 80 years and won't be completed any time soon.

It's Bush House, the headquarters of the BBC World Service. It might look finished, but actually the builders have left a bit off – part of the out-facing capitals of one of the Portland stone columns is not yet in place, leaving an obvious gap. And that gap will never be filled, because the architect, an American called Harry Corbett, deliberately wanted the building to be left 'imperfect' as a nod to the Islamic idea that the notion of man-made perfection is sinful pride and an affront to God.

As if to make up for this missing carving, the head of a Roman marble statue was found during the preparation of the building's foundations, and it is still on display inside. He looks rather cross.

LORD LOVE A DUCK

St James's Park, London's most beautiful, has had a very mixed history in terms of animal welfare. Nowadays, it is home to a large and varied population of waterfowl, including geese, swans, terns, ducks and pelicans. (The pelicans are fed at 2.30pm every day.) In the past, however, they didn't have it so easy.

Plans for the park always involved water in some way, as it is located in an area criss-crossed by 'lost' rivers. The area was originally simply marshland, until it was drained and landscaped by James I, who set up aviaries nearby; hence 'Birdcage Walk'. Charles II was the next monarch to have a crack at landscaping, and his improvements included a long rectangular lake. This lake was very attractive to ducks – fatally so. A duck trap was set up next to the lake, a sort of spur of water which, after a sharp turn, narrowed progressively before ending in a small pond. The narrow section was then covered with netting held up by hoops. Dogs and shots would then be used to drive the ducks out of the lake into this narrow spur where, trapped, they could be clubbed to death. As if that didn't make life hard enough for them, it is said that two crocodiles were also briefly resident in the lake.

This wild population did also give rise to a curious title: Governor of Duck Island. This was a meaningless role, but carried a small stipend and a cottage as a reward for royal favourites. Appropriately, Queen Caroline bestowed the title upon a poet named Stephen Duck.

ST JAMES'S PARK STATION AND 55 BROADWAY

This often-overlooked halt on the District and Circle lines is actually one of the gems of the London Underground network. Above it is the headquarters of London Transport, a purpose-built and rather Gothamesque edifice designed by Charles Holden. On its completion in 1929, it was the tallest building in London. It is also adorned by some very fine modern sculpture, commissioned by Holden from the leading artists of the time (*see below*).

On the ground floor of the building, an early shopping plaza links the station with the street and the entrance to the offices above. Bedecked in marbled stone with high-quality metal fittings and detailing, it's curiously American in feel, reminiscent of Grand Central Station in New York, right down to the signs saying 'To Trains' and the building's address – 55 Broadway.

If you peer through the doors that lead into the Transport for London offices, you'll see to the left a series of machines on the wall that look something like clocks or barometers. These are traffic indicators for the Underground network – a series of paper discs that slowly rotate. As trains pass certain signals, arms on the discs make a mark, so over time you can see what sections of the network are busiest. Sadly, they have been rather neglected in recent years, and admission for the general public to see them up close is now restricted for 'security reasons'.

WINDY SCULPTURE ON 55 BROADWAY

Eric Aumonier: *South Wind*
Jacob Epstein: *Night and Day**
AH Gerrard: *North Wind*
Eric Gill: *East Wind, North Wind and South Wind*
Henry Moore: *West Wind*
Samuel Rabinovich: *West Wind*
Allan Wyon: *East Wind*

* Epstein's contributions were considered shocking by London society in 1929 and caused a scandal that came close to unseating the Underground's managing director. The sculptor soothed the matter over by chiselling two inches off Day's penis. Ouch!

THE HIDDEN PALACE What most tourist guides will tell you is that Inigo Jones's Banqueting House is the only surviving part of Whitehall Palace. They are wrong. The Cabinet Office building – which was recently refurbished – has a long stretch of Tudor brick wall in it, lining one of the corridors of power, and even a couple of rooms, which have been absorbed into the far more recent block. More interestingly, there are still Tudor wine cellars underneath what is now the Ministry of Defence building. Appropriately, considering the survival of the Banqueting House, these cellars are used today for catering and hospitality.

> **The Piccadilly palare/Was just silly slang/**
> **Between me and the boys in my gang/So bona to vada. Oh you/**
> **Your lovely eek and/Your lovely riah.**
> 'Piccadilly Palare', Morrissey

THE MISSING BRIDGE

On the Embankment, by Blackfriars station, there is a very curious sight – a missing bridge. Red-painted Victorian piers still jut from the Thames between the existing road and rail bridges, and the places where the bridge began and ended can still be clearly seen, as can the brightly painted crest of the railway company at the southern end. But they have nothing to support.

Originally, they carried the railway into Blackfriars station. The new bridge was built directly adjacent in an effort to keep trains running as much as possible during works, but when it opened and the time came to remove the old bridge, the engineers made a startling discovery. The bases of the old piers were sunk into the soft bottom of the Thames, and it was feared that the suction effect of removing them would undermine the new bridge. In other words, the old bridge was holding up the new bridge. The piers could not be simply sliced off, either, as that might pose a threat to river traffic. So they had to be kept in place, and are still there today.

Every now and then it is proposed to build a new pedestrian bridge across the old piers, or perhaps even an 'inhabited' bridge like the old London Bridge. But with the wide road bridge so close by, there is little need for such a new crossing. In the meantime, the piers are a popular perching place for the Thames's population of seagulls.

PARLIAMENT SQUARE: THOSE STATUES IN FULL

1. *George Canning* (Richard Westmacott, 1832); from the same sculptor who brought you *Achilles* in Hyde Park, and the pediment of the British Museum.

2. *Lord Derby* (Matthew Noble, 1874); reliefs on the base show the interior of the old House of Commons, before it burnt down in 1834.

3. *Robert Peel* (Matthew Noble, 1876); Noble's second effort for the square.

4. *Benjamin Disraeli* (Mario Raggi, 1883); is that a bathrobe? Not the most practically dressed of PMs.

5. *Abraham Lincoln* (after Augustus Saint-Gaudens, 1920); a recast of the famous statue in Chicago.

6. *Field-Marshall Jan Smuts* (Jacob Epstein, 1956); South African statesman oddly portrayed as an Edwardian ice-skater.

7. *Lord Palmerston* (Thomas Woolner, 19716); poor Woolner had to start all over again when his first statue was too small.

8. *Winston Churchill* (Ivor Roberts-Jones, 1973); famously embellished with turf Mohican during the 2000 May Day protests.

THE DEVIL'S ACRE
Halfway down Victoria Street is New Scotland Yard, the headquarters of the Metropolitan Police, famous for its triangular revolving sign. Thanks to the number of policemen around – now mostly armed – it's possibly one of the safest areas of London, although maybe not if you go round making jokes about terrorism.

This was not always the case. The tangle of narrow streets immediately south of Scotland Yard was called 'the Devil's Acre' in the nineteenth century, as it was one of London's very worst slums, a pit of poverty, crime and despair. Victoria Street was cut through the area as part of an effort to clear the tenements, and the district is still filled with the brick blocks of flats and almshouses built by philanthropists such as George Peabody to better house the slum-dwellers. Also, a good part of the acre has a much more fragrant use now – the headquarters of the Royal Horticultural Society.

THE **MONSTERS** OF MARSHAM STREET

Marsham Street is dominated by Terry Farrell's modern, colourful offices for the Home Office (which featured in the BBC comedy *The Thick of It* as the headquarters of the fictional Department for Social Affairs and Citizenship). These offices stand on the site of Eric Bedford's monstrous Department for the Environment building, which once dominated the area with its three brutal slab-like towers. The Environment building was long reviled as being one of London's most hated structures, ugly to look at and horrible to work in. John Selwyn Gummer, who worked there as Environment Secretary for the Major government, has noted the irony that he was making decisions on urban planning and beautification from a building that should never have been built. Yet Eric Bedford also designed one of London's most loved buildings, the Post Office Tower.

This was also the site of London's first permanent gasworks, which is how it originally came to be used by civil servants – during World War II the concrete base of the gas holder was converted into a bunker to keep administrative workers safe from air raids.

TONY BLAIR IS A *WHAT*?

With the authorities frowning upon graffiti and new legislation that bans unauthorised protests within a half-mile zone of Parliament Square, you'd have thought that the one place that was safe from sloganeering was the very heart of British politics. Well, you'd be wrong.

Tours of the Palace of Westminster are easy to arrange, meaning more than just the MPs get to trudge through the House of Commons. This is just as it should be – they are the people's representatives after all. One thing, however, that isn't mentioned on the official tour concerns the large desk that divides the Government from the Opposition. The desk, a gift from Canada, is covered with worthy-looking tomes, but it's what's

scratched into the desk's surface beneath those books that's really interesting:

'Tony Blair is a c***'

Hard to believe, but it's a fact. Efforts have been made to remove the graffiti, but with only limited time available when the House isn't occupied, the five words have taken some shifting. With the Punch and Judy-style shenanigans that go on in there in the name of British politics it's probably not that surprising to learn of such schoolboy-styled protest, and with the general public under very close scrutiny while they're in the House, suspicion must fall on the MPs themselves. On what side of the desk the scribe responsible sits we leave to your own imagination.

THE WEIRD AND WONDERFUL

Just a selection of some of the more unusual items that have gone under the hammer at Christie's, which is based on King Street.

- A cookie jar once owned by Andy Warhol.
- A collection of exploitation poster art, including 'Slaves in Bondage' and 'Maidens in Uniform'.
- A tom-tom drum used by Paul McCartney in the late 1950s, before The Beatles were even formed.
- A collection of nineteenth-century golf balls.
- A prototype of a *Star Wars* stormtrooper helmet.
- An Elvis Presley concert programme signed by Elvis for Elton John's mum.
- A transcript of a telegram from Marlon Brando to Marilyn Monroe following her nervous breakdown.
- 300 Barbie dolls from the 1960s.
- A prosecution notice demanding that Brian Jones, Bill Wyman and Mick Jagger give statements regarding their lewd and annoying behaviour during a journey on public transport.
- A variety of electric-shock machines.
- A Vivienne Westwood flesh-pink headband with two battery-illuminated green horns.

HORSE FERRIES AND PRISONS ARE SO PASSÉ

Before London Bridge was up (and down and up and down) Horseferry Road was simply the road to the ferry crossing owned by the Archbishop of Canterbury. The only time it wasn't needed was when the Thames froze over, when people could cross the river on foot. This state of affairs carried on until 1734, when it was decided that perhaps a bridge was a good idea. It was all systems go until the plans were changed at the last minute, allowing Westminster Bridge to go up first. By 1862, the horse ferry was obsolete because of the newfangled Lambeth Suspension Bridge.

In the nineteenth century, Millbank Penitentiary was positioned between Horseferry Road and Vauxhall Bridge Road. It was built for the 'lucky' prisoners, both male and female, who weren't to be transported overseas. It started to fall apart even before it was finished and only a year after it opened had to be evacuated due to an outbreak of scurvy. Once it was safe to go back it gained a reputation as the English Bastille, but by the end of the nineteenth century, it had exactly one prisoner left and only two guards.

THE CIVIL SERVICE AND OTHER MISNOMERS

Whitehall, like Fleet Street and Harley Street, is a London thoroughfare that has become synonymous with a profession. In Whitehall's case, that profession is the civil service.

A permanent structure for national government first emerged in the fourteenth century, as a response to the instability caused by the 1348 Black Death and the Hundred Years' War. Setting a pattern for Whitehall projects, the Hundred Years' War overran by 16 years and went considerably over budget.

Whitehall was originally a palace of the same name, which burned down at the end of the seventeenth century, leaving only Inigo Jones's wonderful Banqueting Hall (see also p24).

Bureaucracy, indeed, caused some of Westminster's worst fires. An early system of accounting used 'tally sticks', short lengths of wood that were marked by two parties and then split down the middle. To settle the account, the two halves would have to be reunited.

The tally sticks held by the government were stacked in the basement of the Palace of Westminster. In 1834, they caught fire and burned down most of the building. The construction of the new Palace of Westminster – the one we know today – overran, lasting 30 years or more, and went considerably over budget.

In the twentieth century, the word 'Whitehall' has become associated with stultifying bureaucracy. 'Lift the curtain,' as Enoch Powell once remarked, 'and "the State" reveals itself as a little group of fallible men in Whitehall, making guesses about the future, influenced by political prejudices and partisan prejudices, and working on projections drawn from the past by a staff of economists.'

C Northcote Parkinson was just one of the satirists who attacked the civil service, and in the process he created Parkinson's law, which states: work done is in inverse proportion to the number of civil servants employed; a second law states that public spending rises in order to accommodate the growth in bureaucracy. In other words, civil servants create work where none is needed in order to justify their own existence.

A civil servant inside the Foreign and Commonwealth Office shared one charming insight into Whitehall's internal culture. When the minions of the state get married, they must complete a document called the Marriage Notification Form Section One, or XP7(a). A colleague of this FCO employee decided he wanted to marry his long-time girlfriend, who also worked in the department. So he sent her an email with the notification form attached, and the timeless romantic message: 'Will you XP7(a) me?'

Let's hope the union was on deadline and within budget.

LADIES' BRIDGE

Waterloo Bridge, the longest in central London, is also known as the 'Ladies' Bridge. During World War II, it became associated with tearful partings as troops headed towards Waterloo Station – something exemplified in the 1940 Vivien Leigh tear-jerker *Waterloo Bridge*.

When the war came, however, the bridge was in the process of being rebuilt. Male labour was hard to come by, as most men were off giving Fritz a good hiding, so in consequence it was mostly built by women. It is clad in Portland stone, which has the benefit of being self-cleaning – this was said to be a 'woman's touch' in the design.

> Neanderthalensis stood shivering in Whitehall. It was perishing cold in spite of the declining summer sun. He twitched the woolly rhinoceros skin closer about him and adjusted the pouch, with its lump of iron rations that he had cooked the night before, to lie more comfortably as he plodded on. It would have to last him several days while he looked for another group to join in their hunting. His own had all sickened and died.

Maureen Duffy, *Capital* (1975)

KEEP OFF THE GRASS
ASSORTED THINGS REMOVED FROM GREEN PARK

Lodges	Dislodged
A Library	Unreturned
An Ice House	Melted
The Temple of Peace	Exploded
The Temple of Concord	Also exploded
Deer	Too expensive
The Tyburn Pool	Drained
The Queen's Basin	Demolished
Duelists	Dead
Cars	No parking

ROAD SIGNS, STREETS AND RUNWAYS

This area contains:

- Britain's only right-hand-drive street, outside the Savoy Hotel.

- One of London's oldest street signs, on Marsham Street (it reads 'This is Marsham Street, 1688').

- The Burlington Arcade, where singing, humming and hurrying are forbidden; these rules are enforced by the resident staff of 'beadles'.

- A bridge with a cathedral on it – a figure representing the muse of architecture is on Vauxhall Bridge, and carries a model of St Paul's. Don't fall in the river while leaning over the parapet to see it.

- A large number of painted signs pointing to long-vanished air-raid shelters. There are several examples on Lord North Street.

- ... And a hidden airstrip. The Broad Walk in Hyde Park used to be flanked by elm trees. These were cut down in the 1950s to accommodate the wingspan of a twin-engine Hawker-Siddeley 748, thus providing the Royal Family with a quick way out of London in the event of an imminent nuclear strike.

OUT OF THE LOOP Ever wondered why the northbound platform at the Embankment tube bends so sharply to the right? Of course you haven't – the *Evening Standard*'s doom-laden headlines are distracting enough without having to worry about quirks of underground geography. The thing is, Embankment station's northbound Northern line is situated on the curve of a now disused loop that sweeps round under the Thames and back again. The loop was used to enable trains to reverse while at the same time keeping everything moving, but trains ended up the wrong way round. Despite a turntable eventually being installed at Golders Green the loop was abandoned, and when war loomed in 1938, concrete and rubble was used to plug it up. Apparently in 1939, the plugs were replaced with pressure doors – forward thinking, as the loop was hit by a German bomb and flooded during the Blitz.

DEFINITION OF A HERO

During World War II, Buckingham Palace became an obvious target for the Germans, but despite it being hit seven times there was never any serious damage. The best efforts of the Luftwaffe amounted to nothing more than some broken glass until a hit in 1940, when the palace chapel was destroyed. The Queen responded with typical British self-possession saying: 'I'm glad we have been bombed. Now I can look the East End in the face.'

On 15 September that same year, during the Battle of Britain, a German Dornier bomber made yet another run at the palace and an RAF pilot by the name of Ray Holmes found himself facing off against the enemy plane. The German plane had had engine problems and fallen behind its formation. By the time it had the palace in sight it was burning and two of the crew had bailed out. Holmes, meanwhile, had already engaged several Dorniers and by the time he spotted the limping craft and realised what its target was he was out of ammunition.

Deciding that the only weapon left to him was the Hurricane fighter he was strapped into, Holmes simply rammed the bomber out of the sky.

The impact tore off the tail of the bomber, causing the wings to rip away and leaving the remains of the plane to crash into the forecourt of Victoria station. Holmes later described his encounter with the German bomber as 'a bit of a bump' and for a moment his Hurricane seemed to have survived, but suddenly it fell into a dive and Holmes had no choice but to bail out.

Despite being much too low (only 350ft from the ground) when he opened his parachute, Holmes survived. His chute got snagged on the drainpipe of a house on Ebury Bridge Road and he found himself hanging over a dustbin in the back garden. When he finally hit the ground he saw two girls in the garden next door, and with less hesitation than when he rammed the bomber, he jumped the fence and kissed them both! He was then taken to the local brewery on Pimlico Road to celebrate.

What Holmes didn't know was that his crippled plane had gone on to crash into Buckingham Palace Road at 400mph. It was only in 2004 that, as part of a television programme, what was left of the Hurricane was uncovered by archaeologists. Holmes was on hand to see the remains, which included his old control column, the firing button forever set to FIRE. The engine was also recovered and is now on display at the Imperial War Museum.

Ray Holmes died in 2005.

TRAFALGAR SQUARE
SOHO AND
COVENT GARDEN

TRAFALGAR SQUARE
SOHO AND
COVENT GARDEN

A HUNTING CRY FOR SURE – BUT HUNTING WHAT?

The name Soho was derived from an old hunting call in the days when it was used by Henry VIII as a royal park for the Palace of Whitehall, and it wasn't developed upon until the arrival of James Scott, the first Duke of Monmouth. He was one of the first to build in the area and Monmouth House stood in Soho Square until 1773. Indeed, Soho Square was originally named Monmouth Square until in 1685 the Duke did a silly thing and tried to sit in the throne at the same time as his uncle, James II. His coup d'état in tatters, he was captured and eventually executed at Tower Hill. Eventually, because it took several swipes with the axe to get his head off. The unfortunate duke's adventures continued even after his death when it was realised that no one had bothered to paint his portrait, so he was dug up and his head re-attached for one final sitting.

So what's all this got to do with Soho and hunting? Well, Monmouth Square was renamed King's Square, but admirers of the Duke later renamed it Soho Square in recognition, as *Tallis's Illustrated London* put it in 1851, for 'the word of the day at the field of Sedgmoor' where Monmouth took his last stab at kingship, rallying his dwindling army to pursue the enemy in the same way that they would a hare.

10 THINGS

YOU MAY OR MAY NOT SEE ON THE FOURTH PLINTH OF TRAFALGAR SQUARE ANYTIME SOON

1. Ken Livingstone reading the *Evening Standard*
2. Anything by Banksy
3. David Blaine in a Perspex box
4. The TARDIS
5. A statue of George W Bush
6. A French flag
7. 20ft of mechanical elephant droppings
8. A tourist information stand
9. A public and sincere apology from a politician
10. Something that all Londoners can agree on

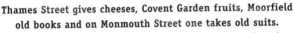

Thames Street gives cheeses, Covent Garden fruits, Moorfield old books and on Monmouth Street one takes old suits.

John Gay, *Trivia, the Art of Walking the Streets of London* (1716)

BONNIE PRINCE CHARLIE

Prince Charles – cheap, fun and with a porn-filled past. No, not 'him', but the cinema just off Leicester Square.

With seats costing as little as £1, the PCC is one of the cheapest forms of entertainment in London. It's also something of a maverick, being the only non-subsidised rep cinema in the whole of the UK. Being 100% independent means it receives no funding from the Arts Council, the Lottery or any other body, depending instead on us paying customers. In exchange they offer up arthouse, classic and cult cinema mixed up with recent Hollywood tosh at prices that are often lower than the popcorn and soft drinks.

That the cinema boasts of its relaxed attitude towards showing banned movies and R-rated material isn't surprising as it was once a porn cinema. But don't worry, it's been completely refurbished since then – though it retains the two-seater love nests on the back row.

It's possible to hire the whole cinema for 400 or so of your closest friends for a movie (or even a PowerPoint demonstration if you are insane), but the PCC really comes into its own during film festivals and the Friday night sing-along-a-movies when customers are encouraged to dress up and play the fool. It's only fair as the management was once happy to let Dom Joly and *Trigger Happy TV* loose on its audience.

COVENT GARDEN – DID YOU KNOW THAT...

...each December a Great Christmas Pudding Race is held? The tradition goes back more than 25 years and raises money for charity.

...the London Transport Museum has an easy-to-read map of the Paris Metro? It was designed by Harry 'London Underground Map' Beck and rejected by the French.

...a ballet featuring a psychopathic dance teacher who kills his pupils was banned from matinée performances? The Royal Ballet deemed *The Lesson* inappropriate for children.

...London's youngest busker was 10 years old? Young Alexander Barnett sang and played guitar to raise money for his stage school fees.

...The Royal Opera House appeared in the film *The Fifth Element*?

...The Piccadilly line route between Leicester Square and Covent Garden is the shortest on the network at 0.16 miles? It's quicker to walk it.

...Alfred Hitchcock was the son of a Covent Garden greengrocer? He made the area home to a serial sex attacker in his film *Frenzy*.

SOHO'S LISTENING POSTS

London is already one of the most remotely observed cities in the world, but soon it could be also the most listened to. Since 2005, Soho's lampposts have been fitted with microphones alongside the more familiar CCTV cameras. The wireless devices initially allowed Westminster Council to monitor noise from the area's many bars and clubs in an attempt to make its war on noise pollution more effective. Now inspectors can monitor any noise complaints as they occur rather than risking turning up when they have finished. Fifty or so wi-fi enabled positions around Soho have also proved beneficial to the police: the new system means that officers can access the CCTV feeds as they patrol rather than waiting for information to be fed back to them.

It's unclear if this also means that Westminster Council now employs retired Cold War agents, more used to listening for Soviet submarines than Soho overspill, to man headphones for the telltale sound of Danny from accounts puking on his shoes. Let's hope the microphones point downwards, as the sounds overheard from the red-lit windows scattered around the area would probably be reminiscent to that of humpback whales.

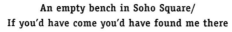

> **An empty bench in Soho Square/**
> **If you'd have come you'd have found me there**
> An inscription in memorial to Kirsty MacColl found on a bench
> in Soho Square, taken from her own song of the same name

FOYLES

Charing Cross Road was famous for its bookshops long before Helene Hanff published *84, Charing Cross Road* in 1970 and, although the number of book stores on the road has dwindled over the years, Foyles has remained longer than most. Indeed it hardly paused for breath as it passed its 100th year of independent trading in 2006.

Its age alone makes the store something of an institution. It is a London landmark, a tourist attraction, a meeting place, a point on the British literary compass and has a long-standing reputation for being 'unique'. Sometimes all this can distract from the fact that it is also a fully functioning modern bookshop, with four floors and a bewildering variety of sections, subsections and book titles.

With over 30 miles of shelving, Foyles is one of the largest bookshops in Europe and feels like a whole series of separate bookstores under one roof. Each section tends to be run in its own way, and the staff themselves do the ordering and title selection. The choice on offer is pretty staggering, especially if you delve deep into the non-fiction sections.

Being a famous bookshop, Foyles has had its share of famous book buyers. Ewan McGregor, Jarvis Cocker and lots of people fitting the description of 'that guy off the telly' are said to often pop in, and Lemmy from Motörhead has been known to haunt the military history section. In the past they've had Henry Miller, JB Priestley, HG Wells, Enid Blyton, Walt Disney, Colonel Gaddafi, Graham Greene, Robert Mitchum, Orson Welles, Ian Fleming, Ingrid Bergman and... well, you get the idea. Richard Burton was quite proud of shoplifting there, and they still hold the slightly dubious record of being the only store to sue the Pope; they thought (mistakenly, it turned out) that he had overlooked a book-club payment.

Part of Foyles-lore is that it used to be a nightmare to shop in. A bizarre payment system involved queueing once with your book in order to obtain a ticket and then again to hand over the ticket along with your payment. Then there was the fact that the books were shelved by publisher instead of author... Londoners with long memories often remark on how much 'fun' it was shopping there back in the 1970s. That all began to change in 1999 when infamous matriarch Christina Foyle died and the store was passed on to her son. In 2002 the beginning of a major shop-wide overhaul took place and space was given over to two other independent businesses forced to close their doors because of rent increases on Charing Cross Road. Foyles now houses feminist bookshop Silver Moon on its first floor, while specialist music store Ray's Jazz now shares space with an independent organic café. This is a great place to sit and drink real coffee while listening to live jazz and glancing at the poor lost souls wandering in and out of the Starbucks across the street.

If you don't mind people scribbling in your books, then Foyles is also a hot spot for meeting authors. They pop in daily, often unannounced, to sign their books and it's quite easy to (literally) bump into the likes of Will Self or Tibor Fischer. Author-focused events as well as the respected Literary Lunches are still very much a part of business as usual and offer a chance for readers to interact with authors such as JG Ballard, Chuck Palahniuk and Douglas Coupland.

Oh and there's a piranha tank. Where? In the children's section, of course...

> I fell into a gloomy and defensive frame of mind. I travelled to Leicester Square and found a cheap café where I got egg and chips for one and sixpence. James Dean had died in a car crash. If a far-sighted destiny would arrange enough accidents of this sort, the world might be left in the hands of really intelligent people, and thus be nearer the millennium.
>
> Colin Wilson, *Adrift in Soho* (1961)

Five names for Soho that failed to catch on

1. **Tally Ho** was too pro fox-hunting
2. **So Ho Tep** was too Egyptian
3. **Crazy Ho** was too Missy Elliot
4. **Ro Bo** was too Japanese
5. **Camel Toe Ho** was too revealing

CYCLO CYCLONE

Pedicab use has boomed in London over the past few years, despite protests from black-cab drivers who see them not only as a rival for drunken fares on a Friday night, but also as yet another slow-moving mode of transport to crush beneath their mighty turning circle. With a few hundred cyclos now vying for space with cyclists, cabs and buses, central London has never been as thrilling a place to be a pedestrian – simply stepping off the kerb is an adventure.

If you do decide to take a pedicab, be sure to agree the fare in advance. The drivers have some serious leg power and you don't want to be on the wrong side of a roundhouse once your journey is over. If you're worried about looking silly while being pulled around the streets by another human being then be sure to wear the shortest skirt possible, along with a comedy L-plate and (probably) fake horns: this tends to be the look of choice for pedicab users and ensures you'll blend in with the weekend traffic.

OSCAR DEUTSCH ENTERTAINS OUR NATION

Today there are numerous multiplexes up and down the country where you can pay good money to see what it is that all the kids are downloading for free. But back in the days when picture houses were still magical places where you could watch Flash Gordon cliffhangers, 'Odeon' was synonymous with the word cinema. This was mostly thanks to one man – Oscar Deutsch.

Even though France and Italy already had their own Odeon chains up and running by the 1920s, Deutsch was a visionary that knew a little spin could go a long way. After opening his first cinema in Birmingham he put it about that Odeon stood for Oscar Deutsch Entertains Our Nation and after that there was no stopping him.

By 1937 there were 250 Odeons across the UK, including the jewel in Oscar's crown – Odeon Leicester Square. The largest cinema in the country to this day, Odeon Leicester Square was built in place of the Alhambra Music Hall, which itself had replaced the Royal Panopticon – a very noble endeavour that did its best to promote science and education, but closed through lack of interest.

Today's Odeon is equipped with state of the art technology, so no matter how poor the movie, at least the sound and image will be crystal clear. It also manages to retain its original feel with both circle and stall seating and a working but seldom used Compton organ. Royalty, as well as nouveau Hollywood types, attend the premieres so the building also has a retiring room for the monarchy. Odds are though that they don't get charged eleven quid a seat.

CARRIE AWAZE II

'Unique' is a word that gets thrown about a lot, but it's no exaggeration to say that having lunch at Carrie Awaze II on Endell Street is an experience that you won't duplicate anywhere else. Moya and Guru love their shop, their menu and their customers. Pop in just the once and you'll be remembered on your return. And return you will.

The atmosphere is straight out of the late 1960s – if you ever wanted to know how Lennon and company felt having their own personal guru then order up a Shankara (chicken vindaloo and dhal sandwich) and have a conversation with the owners. If you're lucky, Guru will play the sitar. The walls are adorned with Indian memorabilia and press cuttings that make for almost as interesting reading as the menu, and mobile phones are frowned upon (you will be asked politely to silence yours if you dare try to ignore the gorgeous food for mundane phone chat).

And rightly so, too. It will be hard to make a selection from the full spread of curries, salads and jacket potatoes (these last treated to individual titles, taken from the names of local streets); but the main draw is the dazzling choice of 50 flavoursome, award-winning sandwiches, each one a meal unto itself.

Close your eyes, take a bite and forget what city you're in.

SOME AWARD WINNING 'DESIGNER' SANDWICHES
FROM
CARRIE AWAZE II

- **Bermuda Triangle** – Tuna, avocado, onion, lettuce, mayonnaise

- **Bayonette** – Bayonne ham, cream cheese, figs

- **Ghengis Khan** – Lamb kebab, onion, chilli, salad, cheese

- **Nervous Actor** – Chicken, ham, honey mustard

- **Brown Bomber** – Onion bhaji, hummus, salad

- **Earthlings** – Curried lentils & spinach, salad, relish

- **Garden of Edam** – Edam cheese, coleslaw, apple, raisins, lettuce

- **Paddie O'Singh** – Curried potato with salad and channa

- **Lambago** – Lamb kebab, salad, onion, relish

- **Snoopy Special** – Peanut butter, banana, apple

> New York City's very pretty in the night-time/
> But oh, don't you miss Soho?

from 'The Boy Looked At Johnny'
by The Libertines (Pete Doherty)

EVERYONE'S OPERA HOUSE

If there's one thing that the Royal Opera House isn't, is stuffy and elitist. Oh hang on... if there are two things that the Royal Opera... oh you get the idea. For a start, since the redevelopment was completed in 1999 the building has been open to the public during the day, meaning you don't need to own a pair of opera glasses or to know a thing about fat women dressed as Vikings to have a look-in. As long as there isn't a special event going on you're free to have a gander at the new Vilar Floral Hall, check out the costumes and take coffee while admiring the views from the Amphitheatre Terrace. There are also free live opera broadcasts that are picked up and relayed on screens throughout the UK.

Even schlocky science fiction is catered to, since the alien opera scenes for Luc Besson's *The Fifth Element* were filmed here. All this is quite fitting, as the Opera House has always had a soft spot for more varied entertainment to run alongside the regular highbrow performances. Back in the eighteenth century the audience risked straining their necks as they watched tightrope walkers, but in 2004 it was most defiantly their eardrums that were in jeopardy as heavy metal icons Motörhead were invited to play – probably in order to ensure that the roof was secure.

MY FAIR LADY: YEAR ONE

These days if you talk to anyone about *My Fair Lady* they'll probably picture the delightful Audrey Hepburn in the lead role or, if their brain cells are misfiring, Martine 'Tiff' McCutcheon. However, despite Julie Andrews now being more recognised for her performances in *The Sound of Music* and *Mary Poppins* it was she in fact who first trod the boards as Eliza Doolittle. Originally playing to great success on Broadway the musical made its London debut, fittingly enough, at the Drury Lane theatre in 1958. Opening night reviews declared the musical a triumph and the crowd went wild, applauding from the moment the curtains opened to reveal St Paul's Church outside Covent Garden. Hundreds of Londoners crowded the streets outside to catch a glimpse of the star-studded audience, which included Ingrid Bergman and Dirk Bogarde. Tickets for the opening night were in such high demand that for the first time ticket touts took to the West End streets asking as much as £5 a ticket (almost a 500% profit) and two sellers were arrested by the police. The show went on to break all box-office records and enjoyed a six-year run in London with almost 3,000 performances. It made a record-breaking £3.5 million as almost four and a half million people watched 'Enry 'Iggins grow accustomed to Eliza's face.

SHOOTING LONDON

FACTS AND FIGURES

In 2005, the total number of days spent filming in London was 12,655. The average number of film crews shooting every day in London is 35.

The 10 most filmed-in boroughs for 2005 were:

1. Westminster – 2231 days
2. Corporation of London – 1051 days
3. Lambeth – 932 days
4. Camden – 891days
5. Southwark – 822 days
6. Wandsworth – 765 days
7. Tower Hamlets –716 days
8. Hackney – 670 days
9. Kensington & Chelsea – 624 days
10. Islington – 527 days

Ten films shot in London during 2005:

Alien Autopsy · *Basic Instinct 2* · *Children of Men* · *The Da Vinci Code* *Love and Other Disasters* · *Notes on a Scandal* · *Scoop* · *Stormbreaker* *Sunshine* · *V For Vendetta*

There are around 70 film festivals in London each year.

THE LEAGUE OF LONDON MEDIA The little faux-Tudor hut in the centre of Soho Square offers a picturesque view on those few days when London is graced by the sun and nearby workers can take a leisurely lunch hour in its company, and it's a favourite building for tourists to snap. It is in fact nothing more interesting than a park-keeper's hut, although fans of 'The League of Gentlemen' did get a glimpse inside when it was featured in their first movie. In *The League of Gentleman's Apocalypse*, Hilary Briss, Herr Lipp and Geoff Tipps use the hut as cover to spy on their own creators in the nearby Tiger Aspect offices. Indeed the square acts as a hub for the media industry, offering an expensive home to Bloomsbury Publishing, the British Board of Film Classification, the Football Association, International Creative Management, the Really Useful Group, the Relevant Picture Company, 20th Century Fox and Paul McCartney's offices. Whether London's media élite also make use of the nearby pubs, clubs, brothels and churches (and in what order) is not known.

STOP THE PIGEON

The war of attrition between the authorities and Trafalgar Square's pigeons continues. The powers-that-be may have any number of schemes up their collective sleeves, but the pigeons always seem to survive and usually find a way to wrap any nearby humans round their little pink feet. With the flock once estimated to number some 35,000 birds that was almost 70,000 little feet; only almost, because feral pigeons tend to suffer from pigeon pox, also known as the dreaded bumble-foot.

It was the sheer numbers of birds that in 2000 resulted in a ban on bird-feed sales, and the numbers dropped to somewhere around 4,500. Trained falcons were also released into the skies above Nelson's Column to police the unruly feathered population. But the mess left behind continued and it was this potential health hazard that in 2003 caused Mayor Ken Livingstone to finally invoke his terrible powers and ban all bird-feeding.

The remaining birds' numbers dwindled down to 700 or so, and their days should have been numbered. But their day was saved by the Pigeon Action Group, who found a loophole in the mayor's new bylaws: it turned out that the feeding ban didn't apply to North Terrace, which is Westminster Council property, and daily feeds were immediately set up. The council of course is looking for a way to stop this, but for now the pigeons (and anything they leave behind) are still very much a part of life in the square.

> **Christmas never does bugger all to Soho.
> It's grey and doomed and hopeless and life-sucking all year round.**
> Warren Ellis, *Planetary, Book Seven* (2000)

COMIC GENIUS TO NOT-SO-COMIC GENIUSES VIA FIVE DEGREES OF SEPARATION ON THE AVENUE OF STARS (COVENT GARDEN)

Charlie Chaplin was the subject of a movie directed by
Richard Attenborough who was in *Hamlet* directed by
Kenneth Branagh who was in *Frankenstein* with
Richard Briers who was in *Spice World* with
Hugh Grant who was in *Love Actually* with **Ant and Dec**

BUT IS IT ART?

If you're open-minded (and don't mind the smell) stepping into an old-fashioned phone booth can be a little like having your own private art and design exhibition – with prostitution as the theme. Despite being illegal from 2001, colourful cards offering sexual services are now more readily found in phone booths than actual working phones are.

The cards began life in the late 1980s as comparatively modest adverts for certain services in and around Soho. As the area became less saucy the ads seemingly went the other way, often with a little photo that left little to the imagination. They are placed there by students or anyone else looking for quick work paid cash-in-hand, and it's difficult to envisage them ever disappearing completely. But a set of cards never stays up for long – it's not just the local council who cart them away, but also tourists and tart card collectors. The cards and their history have been the subject of a design book (*Tart Cards: London's Illicit Advertising Art*) and at least one gallery exhibition.

FAMOUS LOCAL BUSKERS

Billy Bragg · Jon Bon Jovi · Paul McCartney
Badly Drawn Boy · Joe Strummer · Elvis Costello
Jeremy Irons · Paul Bettany · Steve Harley
Shane MacGowan · Rod Stewart

STABBERS

Peter Cook was a comedian so ahead of his time that many are still trying to catch up. Early on in his career, he set up shop in seedy 1960s Soho with The Establishment, London's first 'satirical nightclub', at 18 Greek Street. The American 'comedian's comedian' Lenny Bruce performed there, Barry Humphries and Dame Edna Everage did their thing in its smoke-filled confines, and Frankie Howerd's career was given a much-needed boost there.

The club soon ran into financial difficulties after the failure of a magazine (*Scene*) and an infestation of local gangsters. Cook eventually conceded defeat, later saying, 'I lost interest in business as soon as I went out of business.'

There was still life in Soho for Cook as he stepped in to steer the ailing *Private Eye* magazine. Circulation rose with the help of Humphries's comic-strip adventures of Australian Barry McKenzie in swinging London. Cook was the sole owner of the magazine up until his death in 1995.

BLOOMSBURY
KING'S CROSS
AND HOLBORN

BLOOMSBURY KING'S CROSS AND HOLBORN

TIME FOR A PINT Looking for somewhere cosy, atmospheric and, most importantly, beery, to work your way through our book? Then you could do a lot worse than visiting one of the many famous hostelries Holborn has to offer. Champion of all ale houses is the Cittie of Yorke (22 High Holborn). Three bars, cheap Sam Smith's ale, a mysterious vanishing beer garden and a wanton disregard for accurate spelling make this place a winner. It's particularly beloved of lawyers from the nearby Inns of Court. But don't let that put you off.

Down the road at number 208 is another Sam Smith's pub, the Princess Louise. A genuine display of Victoriana surrounds a bar that takes up more than its share of space. Go upstairs if you want to find a seat. Go downstairs if you want to see some 'interesting' loos.

A trek to the other end of Holborn, armed with a flair for serendipity and access to a military-resolution GPS signal may, or may not, help you to find the Olde Mitre Tavern (Ely Court). It dates from Tudor times, though has been rebuilt. Once again, if you want to sit down, you have to go up – to the ominously named 'Bishop's Room'.

Finally, head to The Lamb on Lamb's Conduit Street (appropriately, served by Young's, whose emblem is a ram). More Victoriana, more cramped drinking space, but bags of charm. You'll be drinking till your head is woolly.

THE QUEEN OF KING'S CROSS

Welcome to King's Cross. Nice, isn't it? Legend says that this was the site of a decisive battle between Roman occupiers and the British tribes. Certainly, the area was known as Battle Bridge for much of its history. Whatever the truth, it's a confrontation you can often see re-created today, as 300 would-be passengers race to clinch the seven unreserved seats on the Edinburgh intercity.

The original battle was supposedly the final campaign of Boudicca (known until a recent re-branding as Boadicea), and there is a rumour that she's buried under platform 9. This rumour is always preceded by the weasel words 'Some guidebooks will tell you...'. Always. Where are these guidebooks? How did this circular nonsense start? Was it something to do with Dan Brown?

Perhaps Boudicca's pagan magic assists Harry Potter and chums on their annual trips to platform nine and three-quarters. You can see a wizardly mock-up if you head towards the space between the two main sheds.

SEX, BOMBS AND ROCK N' ROLL

Visit the Scala in King's Cross, its illuminated white exterior unmissable among the surrounding grime of King's Cross, and you'll see a building which has withstood everything history could throw at it.

Originally the King's Cross Cinema, the place was commandeered before building was even completed, when in 1918 it became an airplane parts factory. It wasn't until 1920 that anyone actually got to watch a film there. Then another world war came along and the cinema was bombed, only to be refurbished and reopened in the 1950s.

In the 1970s the cinema started to cater to a more 'adult audience', which may explain why it soon began to double as a music venue, staging all-nighters so the local speed-freaks could enjoy bands like the Stooges.

Perhaps watching Iggy bound across the stage gave someone an idea because, after it lost its late licence, the King's Cross Cinema became a Primatarium complete with indoor rainforest. Not surprisingly, the monkey house didn't last long and it was back to the films, arthouse this time, until an illegal screening of A Clockwork Orange led to the doors being closed once again.

In March 1999 the Scala reopened after yet another refit. An extra two floors had been added and the building went back to housing bands and club nights. Thankfully there are no plans to bring back the apes.

A HOROLOGICAL HAUNTING
The Dolphin is a charming, if cramped, little boozer skulking on a corner of Red Lion Street. It is unremarkable in all respects except for one: a haunted clock. How a timepiece can harbour ghosts, we don't know. But it's a fact!

In 1915, the pub took a direct hit from a Zeppelin bomb, killing three and injuring many others. But the wounded and dead weren't the only things to be pulled from the rubble. The Dolphin's clock was also salvaged, and given pride of place after the bar was rebuilt. That's despite it being useless; its hands remain frozen at 10.40, the time of the raid.

Bar staff working late at the Dolphin have apparently heard a doleful descending whistle emanating from the clock, as though it's reliving that fatal evening. More likely, it's just one of the aged regulars having an embarrassing gastric episode in the corner. But, hey, the ghost story sells more pints.

> **Northerner, this is your stop. This longhouse of echoing echoes and sooted glass, this goth pigeon hangar, this diesel roost is the end of the line.**
> Simon Armitage, 'King's Cross', in 'From Here to Here: Stories Inspired by London's Circle Line' (2005)

TO THE LIGHTHOUSE

Although mostly set in the Hebrides, Virginia Woolf's famous novel might well have drawn inspiration from much closer to her Bloomsbury home. For on the corner of Pentonville and Gray's Inn Roads stands the world's most incongruous lighthouse. Incongruous and useless. The nearest body of water is the Regent's Canal, not known for its treacherous navigation.

In fact, nobody seems to know what the deuce the tower is for. Or who built it. Or even when it was built. A genuine London enigma.

It's at least 130 years old, as it appears on a print from 1877. But no official records exist as to its origins. Some people have suggested that it was assembled by the nearby Metropolitan Railway, as an eye-catching advertisement for seaside destinations. Others believe that it was just an ad hoc bit of joinery, assembled by a local shopkeeper. One account even speaks of the folly emitting a bluish light, as a celebration of the 1924 British Empire Exhibition. Ironic, really, in such a famous red-light district.

UNDERGROUND RAIL
BUT NOT AS WE KNOW IT

The tube lines aren't the only tracks running under Holborn. If you go to the corner of Theobalds Road and Southampton Row, you'll be standing very close to two subterranean rail systems.

The first, and most obvious, is indicated by a set of tracks heading down under Kingsway. They're gated off and inaccessible today, but once formed the northern end of a double-decker tram system that ran right down to the river. After the tram line closed in the 1950s, the underpass was repurposed, rather counter-intuitively, as a flood-warning nerve centre for London. Since the building of the Thames Barrier, however, the northern sections have remained largely redundant except as a storage area for road-works equipment (the southern sections have been converted into a road underpass). These gated tracks recently appeared as the entrance to a secret base in the film *The Avengers*.

The second railway on this corner is much deeper. For nearly 100 years, the Royal Mail shunted post across the capital on its own miniature underground railway. The line passes very close to the Kingsway tunnel, heading south-west from the Mount Pleasant sorting office towards New Oxford Street. Sadly, the system was closed down in 2003 for financial reasons.

Mix in the Piccadilly line and a major east-west sewer, and it's all very crowded underneath this junction.

SELECTED GRADUATES FROM UNIVERSITY COLLEGE LONDON

Ricky Gervais, comedian (2:2 in philosophy after dropping out of biology)

Jonathan Dimbleby, TV presenter (philosophy)

Brett Anderson, singer (architecture)

Justine Frischmann, singer (also architecture; a connection is made)

Antony Gormley, sculptor (erm, sculpture)

Jonathan Ross, TV presenter (history)

The whole of Coldplay (Chris Martin: a first in ancient world studies)

Chris Nolan, film director (English literature)

Rachel Whiteread, sculptor (art)

Mahatma Gandhi (law)

WHERE, OH WHERE, IS REGENT SQUARE?

Over near Regent's Park, surely? Somewhere in the unlearnably complex grids of Marylebone or Fitzrovia? But no. Regent Square is in fact a quirky and little-visited patch between King's Cross and Bloomsbury. Time to make it more popular. Get out your *A-Z* and track the place down, for there's nowhere quite like it in London.

For starters, its gruesome story rivals that of the Ripper's Whitechapel. In 1893, a jilted man shot his one-time fiancée and her new beau there before turning the pistol on himself. Twenty or so years later, a grisly package was discovered there containing a female torso whose legs were enclosed in a second parcel close by. No sign of the arms and head. Later horrors came in the Blitz, when most of the square was destroyed, including two landmark churches.

Today the place is anonymous. But look closer and feel the oddness. For starters, can you see any birds? Never. They don't perch here for some reason. The only avians you'll spot are nailed down to the central plane tree. And, then, what's with that bollard in the north-east corner? What the hell is it for? And the writing on the wall, and the curious disused barrier, and the peculiar graveyard to the south. What are you waiting for? Go have a look.

LONDON: WHERE THE STREETS ARE PAVED WITH... IRON DISCS

Bloomsbury, with its elegant streets and squares, is a cracking place to look for coal-hole covers. What? No, wait... come back. Seriously, these things are more interesting than you might think. Just put on your nerd hat for a few minutes. Trust us.

The little buggers can be found lurking outside many Georgian or Victorian houses. You've probably seen countless examples, without realising. You know, those little discs of iron decorated with intricate, geometric patterns. They're everywhere. Until the 1960s, these were used like fuel caps on cars; gently lifted by the coal man, who'd deposit a weekly scoop of the black stuff direct into his customer's basement. Then came central heating and clean-air acts, and the age of coal was over.

Today, the cast-iron covers are functionless pieces of street furniture, largely unheeded by the millions of people who tramp over them every day. But they're still ubiquitous, and many different patterns can be found. So put on your best anorak, and take up a new hobby: coal-hole spotting. Now you know about them, you won't be able to resist looking.

> King's Cross has always had a name for prostitution, and where there are brasses there's always smack; and nowadays if you're anywhere in London where there's smack, then there will be crack as well. The two go together like foie gras and toast.
>
> Will Self in the *Evening Standard* (September 1991)

WHY'S IT CALLED THAT?

1. **Bloomsbury:** After William de Blemund, a medieval landowner, whose estates were known as Blemondesberi. They weren't fussy about spelling in those days.

2. **King's Cross:** Named after an hilariously unpopular statue of George IV. It only stood for a handful of years, but these coincided with the building of the rail station, so the name stuck.

3. **Holborn:** From Old English *holh-burna*, meaning valley stream. Refers to the upper stretch of the River Fleet.

4. **Southampton Row:** After the Earls of Southampton, who owned Bloomsbury Manor.

5. **Lamb's Conduit Street:** William Lambe, a wealthy philanthropist, built a conduit on land around here as a source of fresh water.

6. **Tavistock Square/Place:** Named after the Marquess of Tavistock, the title given to the eldest son of the Duke of Bedford.

7. **Theobalds Road:** A former royal track that led to the Stuart kings' hunting grounds at Theobalds Park, Hertfordshire.

8. **Boswell Street:** Not named after the famous biographer of Samuel Johnson, but a local bricklayer who built houses in this area.

9. **Great Ormond Street:** named for the first Duke of Ormonde, a Civil War commander of the Royalist persuasion.

10. **Kingsway:** Was going to be called Queensway. Unfortunately, Victoria died before its completion and the name was changed to salute the new king.

A **SQUARE** DANCE

Bloomsbury is famous for its elegant squares. But to the newcomer, they all tend to blend into one. Here are some little factlets to help you out:

Russell Square: The watchword here is 'big'. This is London's most sizeable square garden and contains the largest central hotel (the Royal National, which can house 3,000 guests).

Bedford Square: Easily the most stylish of the squares. It contains the greatest number of blue plaques – six of them, no less.

Tavistock Square: London's peace square, with memorials to conscientious objectors, the Hiroshima victims and Mahatma Gandhi.

Gordon Square: Twin of Tavistock Square. Once home to neighbours and, no doubt, lovers Virginia Woolf and Lytton Strachey.

Bloomsbury Square: First of the squares, built in the 1660s. The entry/exit ramps to its underground car park curve eccentrically to avoid tree roots.

Queen Square: The place where howling-mad George III was treated for his illness. The Queen's Larder pub takes its name from his queen, who stored his favourite foods in its basement.

Mecklenburgh Square: Obscure but sizeable private square to the east. Not many features of interest, but keep an eye out for a little-known short cut through the Foundling Estate in the north-west corner.

Brunswick Square: On the other side of that short cut. The only Bloomsbury Square from which you're likely to see sheep. Neighbouring Coram's Fields contains a small children's farm.

Regent Square: Least elegant, but most fascinating of all the squares. Murders, mutilations, bombings and strange artworks. *See p56* for all the gory details.

Woburn Square: The smallest of the Bloomsbury Squares. Along with Torrington Square, it is now almost entirely given over to university buildings.

HOLBORN'S HIDDEN BUNKER

There's a curious wooden monolith at the southern end of Leather Lane, just before this market street meets High Holborn. Sitting on the base of the structure, you can often feel the warm breath of ventilated air. But what's it ventilating?

Deep beneath the streets of Holborn is a labyrinth of tunnels and rooms, never open to the public. They started life as deep-level shelters, excavated during World War II but completed too late to be of much use. After the war, the tunnels were to be linked with others around London to build a high-speed tube network. However, the money never appeared and the complex was acquired and expanded by the General Post Office, who turned it into a vast subterranean telephone exchange. Rumour has it that a secret governmental bunker was also installed at the eastern end, close to where the ventilation shaft must lead.

The only visible entrance to the facility can be found at 32 High Holborn. A dusty, anonymous door with no signage leads into the vacant back rooms of the former Chancery Lane ticket hall. It's said that the complex is now completely decommissioned. But sometimes, sitting on the ventilation shaft and feeling the hot air streaming out, pondering the unseen warren deep below, one wonders what Ernst Stavro Blofeld and James Bond are up to these days.

PUTTING THE 'ARCH' BACK INTO 'MARCHING ORDERS'

Many old London landmarks are, sadly, no longer with us (Crystal Palace, Old London Bridge, Westminster Aquarium). Saddest of all, though, is the Euston Arch, a huge Doric portal from 1838 that once guarded the entrance to the eponymous station.

Warning: pedantic digression time. Like many of London's great structures (Canary Wharf, Post Office Tower, the Gherkin, NatWest Tower), Euston Arch goes by a misnomer. There were no arches in the Euston Arch, and it would more properly be called a propylaeum (a giant pedimented entrance). But as that sounds more like a jet fuel, we'll stick with calling it an arch.

The whole edifice was dismantled in the 1960s to make way for a new station concourse and a drab Richard Seifert office complex (see also Centrepoint, NatWest Tower, King's Reach). What were they thinking? A small reminder of former grandeur remains, however. Twin Portland stone lodges from 1869 still front Euston Road, engraved with their lists of train destinations. Thank goodness we now live in more enlightened times, when London icons aren't needlessly eradicated (erm, see also Routemaster buses, Wembley towers...).

HOLBORN: WHO? WHAT? WHERE? WHY?

Holborn is a baffling place to the uninitiated. Like London as a whole (*see p94*), it's a fiendishly slippery concept to define, and even its pronunciation, frankly, can be a bit of a bugger.

So what is it? Just another part of London? Oh no, there's far more to it than that. Holborn can variously refer to:

1. The area as a whole;
2. Its tube station;
3. A former metropolitan borough;
4. The main road running through the area;
5. The tributary of the 'lost' river Fleet, which once flowed through it; and
6. A type of tobacco associated with the locale.

So, now we've got it down to six definitions, the next question is: where do you find it? Well, Holborn straddles the boundaries of Camden, Westminster and the City, steadfastly refusing to side with any of them. It forms the snug buffer zone betwixt City and West End; a small area of no-man's land, to which neither tourists nor Londoners gravitate. And at weekends, it is a ghost town.

The next puzzle of Holborn is how to pronounce it. The trick here is to use the fewest number of syllables possible. If you're determined to sound like a tourist, say 'hole-bourne'; if you want sound like one of the rapidly vanishing locals, however, say 'ob'n'. Likewise, Theobald's Road, the other main east-west thoroughfare, takes the vernacular 'Tibbald's Road'.

For those sensitive to the character of an area, Holborn also presents problems. The City is full of guffawing City-types, Covent Garden has a touristy jingle about it, Camden is bohemian and smelly, Clerkenwell is a mecca for skrimshanking white twentysomethings who smoke pot and design things. Holborn, meanwhile, struggles to find its soul. An incoherent admixture of office workers, bandaged children, third-generation Italian immigrants, lawyers, hobos and publishers. Oh, and Cherie Blair, whose chambers are here.

Where Holborn begins and where it ends also differ according to whom you speak to. Does Lincoln's Inn count? West of Kingsway? North of Theobalds? Who can say? Perhaps the situation can best be described by paraphrasing the great Alan Partridge: Holborn is an attitude.

> Before leaving home I'd checked the traffic cameras on the BBC local news, and as ever the one pointed down Euston Road depicted a poorly laid-out yet astonishingly popular car park.
>
> Tim Moore, *Do Not Pass Go* (2003)

SOME VAGUELY APPROPRIATE BLOOMSBURY ANAGRAMS

Coram's Fields	*Older fascism*
Bloomsbury Group	*Bulbous Orgy Romp*
Gower Street	*Swot greeter*
Lamb's Conduit Street	*Battled Consumerist*
Euston Road	*Auto Drones*
Tottenham Court Road	*Hotrod toucan matter*

---

10 WAYS TO LIVEN UP A TRIP TO THE BRITISH MUSEUM

1. Dress up as a Victorian Imperialist. Wander the galleries recounting to strangers how you rescued all this stuff from the savages.

2. Fall to your knees in front of the mummy cabinets, clutch your throat and cry 'Dear God, the legends were true! Run!'

3. Wear a long, red wig and sprawl naked on the glass roof. See if anyone gets the obscure satirical reference.

4. Leave behind a tablet of 'cave art' depicting a hairy man with a shopping trolley. And then see how long it takes before people notice. Oh, Banksy already did that.

5. Loudly threaten to scrawl over the priceless Roman marbles with indelible marker pen, then look outraged when the guards start running.

6. Ask in the Reading Room if they've got Jordan's biography.

7. In the gift shop, insist that your change be given in Carolingian coinage. Preferably silver denarius.

8. Find the dullest of the many dull potsherds on display. Wave your arms excitedly while uttering exclamations of amazement under your breath. Then tell anybody who enquires that you've tracked down a fragment of Christ's chimney.

9. Dress up as C3PO out of *Star Wars* and march up to the Sutton Hoo helmet. Place your hands on the glass cabinet and, with all the pathos a robot can be expected to muster, whisper the word 'Father'.

10. Go up to one of the attendants, all excited, and say: 'Hey, I've got this really great joke. You'll never have heard it. How much, right, does a Grecian earn? No... no, that's not right. I mean, what's a Grecian urn? Eh?... Eh? Depends what his job is, yeah? Ha!'

BLOOMSBURY BONKING

It's a famous adage that the bookish Bloomsbury group of toffo socialites lived in squares and loved in triangles. Whoever invented that cliché patently had a simpleton's grasp of geometry. Try drawing a diagram of who shagged who and you'll see what we mean. Ginny Woolf and chums were so promiscuous, you end up with something like the wiring diagram for Piccadilly Circus. Forget love triangles. We're talking seven-dimensional hyperspheres here.

But let's give it a go. Get a pencil and paper ready and prepare to draw out a cat's-cradle of adultery, buggery and ménages-à-cinq.

Let's get things going with Virginia Woolf (and lots of people did). Despite marriage to Leonard Woolf, she enjoyed occasional rumpy-pumpy with friend and writer Vita Sackville-West, daughter of Baron Sackville. Vita was also married and took other lesbian lovers, including Violet Keppel (a possible illegitimate daughter of Edward VII and great-aunt of Camilla Parker-Bowles).

Going back a step, Virginia also had amorous encounters with, and a marriage proposal from, writer Lytton Strachey. Now this is where it gets complicated, so sharpen your pencil. Strachey forged a long-term relationship with painter Dora Carrington. Dora's husband, Ralph Partridge, didn't mind. He was also bedding Strachey. The three even went on honeymoon together. Dora also fell madly in love with Henrietta Bingham, daughter of the American ambassador and erstwhile bed-mate of, you guessed it, Lytton Strachey. Oh, and Strachey's niece also got in on the action from time to time.

Got it so far? Well, that was but an easy warm-up. It's time now to consider Vanessa, Virginia's more promiscuous sister. Vanessa married art-critic Clive Bell and had two children by him. Despite motherly responsibilities, the inevitable affairs ensued. After dumping her artist-lover Roger Fry, she hooked up with Duncan Grant, a well-known and well-bedded homosexual (and, you couldn't make this up, a cousin of Lytton Strachey). They had a daughter, Angelica. Until adulthood, Angelica had always believed her father to be Clive Bell. When she found out the truth, she acted as any proper Bloomsburyite would by marrying David Garnett, one of her true-father's lovers and 25 years her senior. Just to complete the tangled web, Duncan Grant was also the lover of the great economist John Maynard Keynes, and had a relationship with Adrian Stephen, the brother of Virginia and Vanessa.

It's a wonder they ever found the time to write or paint anything.

LITTLE ITALY

A few traces of the large Italian population that once lived here:

1. Sicilian Avenue. An elegant and distinctive arcade of shops and cafés, lined with Sicilian marble.

2. Italian Church of St Peter, Clerkenwell Road. A little-known building of incredible beauty dating from 1863.

3. Italian Hospital, 40 Queen Square. Opened by Giovanni Ortelli in 1884 to treat the poor immigrant community. The hospital closed in 1989, but still bears prominent signage.

4. Mazzini-Garibaldi Club, Red Lion Street. Opened in 1861, the dusty drinking den is famously never open.

5. 183 Gower Street. A blue plaque marks the former home of Giuseppe Mazzini, a political radical and 'prophet' of a unified Italy.

6. 10 Laystall Street. Another plaque to Señor Mazzini. Not a blue one, but it does have a small relief of the patriot's face.

7. 5 Hatton Garden. A third plaque to the itinerant Mazzini.

8. 17 Red Lion Square. Pre-Raphaelite painter Dante Gabriel Rossetti shared his home, and his blue plaque, with two other notables (Edward Burne-Jones and William Morris).

THE PRIME MINISTER, THE ASSASSIN AND THE WHOLLY UNCONNECTED FOOTBALL TEAM

To the west of Lincoln's Inn Fields stands a gorgeous seventeenth-century house painted in Arsenal's home colours. Although presumably nothing to do with the Gunners, the house does have an unfortunate connection with guns.

The building's most famous resident, as noted on a plaque, was one-time PM Spencer Perceval. This embattled statesman had to contend with Luddite riots, royal insanity and a cabinet of nincompoops (some things never change), but is mostly noted as the only British prime minister to be shot: on 11 May 1812, the unfortunate leader was gunned down in Westminster Palace by disgruntled merchant John Bellingham. He too met his end a week later, courtesy of the hangman's noose. Perceval is now buried in Charlton, just a short walk from Arsenal's original ground.

In an interesting footnote, Bellingham and Perceval's modern-day descendants also had a political squabble. During the 1997 General Election, Henry Bellingham and Roger Percival both fought for the constituency of Norfolk North West, although neither man won.

REGENT'S PARK
AND CAMDEN TOWN

REGENT'S PARK
AND CAMDEN TOWN

TV-AM RIP In the heady days of 1981 an old Henley's garage between Hawley Crescent and the Grand Union Canal was chosen to house a radical new idea – breakfast television. Although the BBC managed to pip ITV to the post by launching its own pre-9am pre-emptive strike with *Breakfast Time*, *TV-am* launched a few months later, and where the BBC had Frank Bough and Russell Grant, ITV had giant eggcups. In fact the eggcups are about all that remain now: *TV-am* made its last broadcast on 31 December 1992 and the building fell into the hands of MTV, who kept the cups.

Sir Terry Farrell of Charing Cross Station fame designed the building, including the huge lettering jutting out of the side and the rainbow arch. This arch must have brightened up the picket lines during a technicians' strike in 1987 and ensuing six-month lock-out by management, during which TV-am was forced to rerun the 1960s *Batman* TV show and other fillers. Oddly enough, the theme tune 'Good Morning Britain' was composed by Jeff *War of the Worlds* Wayne. Kind of fitting as Timmy Mallet on *Wacaday* was at least as disturbing as waking to a Martian invasion.

DON'T LOOK NOW

There are not many places in London that aren't safe, but one area to be 'very' careful of is the western end of the Regent's Canal. Here you're in terrible danger of falling over into Little Venice. It's chic and fashionably expensive, and it's easy to make the wrong assumption that it gained its nickname from the fact that if you squint (or are highly medicated) you can fool yourself that you're actually in Venezia. This is a recognised medical condition called Venetian Blindness. Once in this fugue state it's just a matter of time before you get picked off by one of the red-waterproofed evil dwarves that patrol the area and help keep the property prices high by attacking any riff-raff that gets too close. To this day, each time you order a Veneziana at Pizza Express the company donates 25p that goes to help the victims of these malicious little buggers.

THE **X** FACTOR

simplicity is the legendary Deutsch extension that was built as a Möbius Strip and disappeared in December 1950, reappearing briefly every seven years to allow some very confused passengers off (if you've read AJ Deutsch's *A Subway Named Mobius*, 1950, you'll know what I mean).

If the London tube map fell into the hands of seventeenth-century pirates the odds are they'd act not very differently from modern-day Italian tourists: standing on the wrong side of the escalators, getting confused at Bank and dressing more sharply than your average Londoner. One place that would get them very excited though is Camden Town. X marks the spot after all.

You see, Camden Town is that rare station that, like William Wallace, manages to go in four different directions at once. This is a great feat, considering the station is served by a single black line. The only part of the tube network more confusing in its

Another X for our buccaneering tourists to get excited about is above ground, at the crossroads of Camden High Street, Parkway, Camden Road and Kentish Town Road. This was once the site of many a public hanging, but these days the spot acts as the point where first-time visitors turn their maps around and realise they're walking away from the market.

Which funnily enough is itself an ex (see what we did there?) timber yard.

TOMB IT MIGHT CONCERN

The burial ground of St Pancras Old Church is full of curiosities, from the sinister Hardy Tree to the Gothic sundial commemorating a literal graveyard shift.

Centre stage, however, is what appears to be a giant, sunken telephone box made from stone. And it is here that two of Britain's greatest architects are historically fused.

This is the family tomb of Sir John Soane (he of the eponymous museum). It was designed in 1815 by Soane himself, and is described by Pevsner as 'extremely Soanesque, with all his originality and all his foibles'. And all

his snakes and pineapples, judging by the decoration.

Over 100 years later, Giles Gilbert Scott was musing over suitable designs for a new telephone kiosk. He wanted something slightly old-fashioned and distinctive, to make people more comfortable with the scary new technology, and remembered the strange tomb from St Pancras. London's famous red phone boxes were the result. Scott, of course, went on to design Bankside and Battersea Power Stations. Which in turn have influenced everyone from Pink Floyd to Dr Who. And so the baton is passed.

CAMDEN: WHERE YOU CAN ALWAYS FALL BACK BEHIND THE PUB BATTLEMENTS ON A FRIDAY NIGHT

● **Caernarvon Castle** NW1 8AA – 246 miles (about 6 hours 1 min) away from Caernarfon.

● **The Dublin Castle** NW1 7AN – 359 miles (about 8 hours 19 mins) away from Dublin.

● **The Eastnor Castle** NW1 1NR – 144 miles (about 3 hours 21 mins) away from Eastnor.

● **Edinboro Castle** NW1 7RU – 437 miles (about 9 hours 12 mins)

away from Edinburgh, though the spelling's different.

● **Pembroke Castle** NW1 8JA – 246 miles (about 5 hours 38 mins) away from Pembroke.

● **Windsor Castle** NW1 4SH – 27 miles (about 45 mins) away from Windsor.

● **Roy Castle** – OK, we made that one up but there is a pie and mash shop called Castle's.

BLOW-UP BRIDGE

On 2 October 1874, the animals of London Zoo were rudely awoken by the most powerful explosion ever recorded in the capital up to that point. For reasons never fully explained, a barge laden with gunpowder and petroleum had detonated on the Regent's Canal beneath the Macclesfield Bridge – one of the northern entrances to Regent's Park – devastating the area. It spelt tragedy for the three crew members, who were killed instantly. More fortunate were a troupe of rare birds who escaped to freedom after their zoo cages were blown open.

The canal was reopened a few days later. The bridge was soon rebuilt using the original cast-iron columns, which were surprisingly free of damage. You can still see them today. Although there's no sign of blast damage, there are a number of deep grooves worn into their outer faces. These were carved long ago by harness ropes rubbing against the insides of the columns. When the bridge was rebuilt, the columns were turned around, so now the grooves face outwards.

> **I once did a gig for Save the Whales, did alright, must have saved loads of them. Then I got mugged in Camden, and not one of them turned up to help!**
>
> Craig Charles, commenting during the Ride the Wave game for the UK version of Japanese show *Takeshi's Castle*

IT'S NOT ALL WOOLF AND DICKENS YOU KNOW

Despite what the guidebooks say, it is possible to find some literary connections to this area that don't have to do with either Virginia or Charlie.

The Euston Road, for example, features heavily in the fantastic *Twenty Thousand Streets Under the Sky* by Patrick Hamilton, while Primrose Hill is the setting for two very different tales: everyone's favourite spotty dog story, *101 Dalmatians*; and everyone's favourite Martian apocalypse story, *War of the Worlds*.

And while we're on the sci-fi, if you pick up a copy of William Gibson's novel *Pattern Recognition* you'll find plenty of mentions of Camden Town, as you will in any of the Christy Kennedy mysteries penned by Peter Charles.

One of the weirdest examples of NW1 literature, though, has to be Robert Rankin's *Apocalypso*, which features alien vegetables and the all-powerful Ministry of Serendipity at Mornington Crescent.

THE ROUNDHOUSE

The Roundhouse began life back in 1847 as nothing more thrilling than a simple turntable engine shed, before being leased to a distiller who used it as a gin warehouse and production facility for the next 90 years or so. By the 1960s things were due a bit of a shake-up and it was converted into the ominous-sounding Centre 42 – named after an arts-friendly resolution passed by the Trades Union Congress. April 1966 saw the venue used by CND, with Jeff Beck and The Yardbirds among the first in a very long list of bands to play there. It was the *International Times* launch party in October of that year that really kicked things into high gear, with Pink Floyd providing the tunes and Yoko Ono doing her arty thing. Other all-nighters followed that saw just about every influential band from the late 1960s/ early 1970s take the stage. Whether they'll all remember it is another matter, as trying to work out if the sugar cubes had been laced with LSD was just one of the eccentricities on offer.

The Roundhouse was also a perfect fit for theatre, as director Peter Brook's productions proved. One was somewhat too successful when a stage invasion of *Paradise Now* by the audience led to the nude actors hiding behind police officers, who raided the building and cited the audience for being in direct contravention of the Greater London Council's fire regulations. Other onstage chaos included: more nudity in *Oh Calcutta!* (with Tony Blair's father-in-law), an Andy Warhol performance that inspired a David Bowie song, and trapeze artists falling from the rafters. As if all that wasn't enough, an appearance by the Ramones helped the British punk scene to find its feet, and a new generation of bands and fans called the Roundhouse home.

This lasted only until the late 1970s, when a reduced crowd capacity, coupled with noise complaints, saw the Roundhouse shake off its musical heritage and concentrate on theatre. By 1983 it was closed, but it survived several demolition attempts to reopen in 1998 with the formation of the Roundhouse Trust. There followed a run of acclaimed productions, and then an ambitious redevelopment plan.

Perhaps the most recent controversy surrounding the Roundhouse came in 2002, when Michael Moore held a very successful one-man show in which he aimed comedic spleen at George W Bush. On one eventful evening the show was delayed, only for Moore eventually to take the stage and claim he was the target of white supremacists who had threatened his life. Thankfully he still found time to make fun of Americans.

MISSION: IMPROBABLE

Sir Edmund Berry Godfrey's body was discovered at Primrose Hill on 17 October 1678 after he had gone missing five days earlier; he had been run through with his own sword. No regular murder, this, as the resulting inquest discovered that Godfrey was murdered elsewhere, strangled and stabbed post mortem. Obviously it was the work of the Pope...

You see Godfrey, a well known London magistrate and friend of Samuel Pepys, had been told of a plot in which the ironically named Pope Innocent XI was conspiring to overthrow both British King and government. The convoluted plan involved Charles II being shot by Spanish Jesuits, stabbed by four Irishmen and poisoned by the Queen's physician. Just for the hell of it, the Protestants were to be massacred and Ireland was to be invaded by the French.

Hit spy-fi shows like *Alias* and *24* were still a long way off, so rumours such as these were all the general population had for entertainment. No sooner had the plot become public knowledge that Godfrey disappeared and the country went nuts. Once the body was found poor Godfrey became an anagram – 'Dy'd by Rome's reveng'd fury' – and the subject of a commemorative dagger, inscribed with 'Remember the murder of Edmund Berry Godfrey' on one side and 'Remember religion' on the other. Some 3,000 were sold in a single day.

This nonsense held sway for a number of years, with conspiracy landing atop conspiracy about the 'Popish Plot' and scores of people being executed. For the murder of Godfrey three men were eventually strung up on Primrose Hill, which was known at the time as Greenberry Hill. Their names were (*dun dun dah!*) Green, Berry and Hill.

JUST SOME OF THE ROUNDHOUSE PLAYERS

David Bowie, The Rolling Stones, **Elton John**, The Who, **Cream**, The Move, **Led Zeppelin**, Motorhead, **Fleetwood Mac**, John Lee Hooker, **Pink Floyd**, The Doors, **Cat Stephens**, 999, **T. Rex**, Deep Purple, **The Clash**, Kraftwerk, **the Stranglers**, Jimi Hendrix, **The Jam**, The Damned, **Elvis Costello**, Adam and the Ants, **Sham 69**, the Ramones, **Incredible String Band**, Soft Machine, **Jefferson Airplane** and The New Philarmonic Orchestra. The Sex Pistols only ever rehearsed here.

10 THINGS YOU WON'T SEE AT THE MCC MUSEUM AT LORD'S

1 The unfeasibly long beard of WG Grace. The famous cricketer and silent partner in the Grace Brothers Department Store bequeathed his facial hair to slum children who, according to the *Evening Standard*, 'spent it on drugs'.

2 Mr S Liver, who was 'bowled out' by Jehangir Khan in 1936 along with a sparrow. The bird was stuffed and put on display, while Mr Liver was just pushed under the pavilion where no one could see.

3 A googly – even dimmer relative to the dodo. Was used by cricketers on long sea voyages, usually after the last real ball was knocked for six. The googly had the added benefit of flying back once hit. Now extinct.

4 Women's cricket memorabilia. Girls can't play cricket, stupid.

5 The cricket bat used by Simon Pegg in *Sean of the Dead*. It's too cool to be left gathering dust in a stuffy sporting museum.

6 Visitors wearing iPods – the only tune allowed to be played within the catchment area of Lord's is 'Soul Limbo' by Booker T & the MG's.

7 Wicket Wysrti Warrick (although it sounds very crickety this was actually the Ewok in *Return of the Jedi* played by Warwick Davis).

8 Anything to do with Gamma Cricket or 'real' cricket. Despite being played for hundreds of years the game is still in 'beta', ergo 'test' cricket. It's hoped that when the game is finally out of beta it will be a lot shorter and more exciting.

9 The 1988 Botham Report. The governmental report was personally whitewashed by Margaret Thatcher over worries it would affect British morale to learn that cricket was a silly game that no one, least of all the players, understands.

10 This page of *The London Collection* – no sense of humour these sporty types.

> There's a great crowd of tourists/
> And they're coming down the street/
> Pleased as punch with brand new Doc Martens on their feet/
> Past stalls of leather jackets, old bric a brac/
> Indian sunglasses or a Chinese bobble hat
>
> 'Camden Town', Suggs

YOU'LL PICK IT UP AS WE GO ALONG

After the comedian, cartoonist and actor Willie Rushton died in 1996, a plaque was erected to commemorate his life in the ticket office of Mornington Crescent tube station.

Rushton did not live near Mornington Crescent, and nor was he a particularly big fan of London's transport system, but he had helped to create one of the most ingenious, intoxicating and pleasurable parlour games in the world, which just happens to share its name with the Northern line station.

Invented by Rushton and his colleagues on Radio 4's quiz game *I'm Sorry I Haven't A Clue*, Mornington Crescent may seem a little complicated to the uninitiated but it's really a very simple matter: you advance one station along the tube map at a time until you are able to announce your arrival at 'Mornington Crescent'. Of course it is always useful to familiarise yourself with the Einstein/Tchaikovsky rule of 1963 regarding Fenchurch Street before you go up against an experienced player, and bear in mind that you should never perform a Queen's entry without first opening a King's passage.

A ZED AND TWO NOUGHTS PART 1

JUMBO

London Zoo, while not having a record as bad as Mr Chinnery, the veterinarian from *The League of Gentlemen*, did occasionally not have the firmest grip on its guests. Take Jumbo for example. Born in the Sudan and then holidaying in France for a spell, this African elephant came to London Zoo in 1865, famously taking Londoners to his huge heart by allowing them to ride around on his back rather than picking them up with his trunk and throttling them.

The London zookeepers couldn't get their tongues around the word 'jambo' (Swahili for 'hello') so instead called him Jumbo. The poor chap would probably have lived longer if they'd kept him, but unfortunately he was sold on to PT Barnum.

Under Barnum's care Jumbo was crushed to death by a train in Ontario. Legend has it that this was the result of a rescue attempt to save a younger elephant, proving that there really is one born every minute.

After his death Jumbo was stuffed and might well have been with us still if the Americans hadn't managed to set fire to him. By 1975 all that was left was his tail and a small pile of ashes, now stored securely in a peanut butter jar. Thanks to Barnum the word 'jumbo' is today synonymous with anything huge.

NIGHT CRAWLERS

A pub crawl is an odd experience, as the better a time you have at each stop the less you remember the next day. A gig crawl is a much better proposition. But what are the odds of finding enough different bands taking different stages at different times and all the venues being within staggering distance of each other? Better than you think, if you partake in the annual Camden Crawl.

The Camden Crawl started in 1995 and ran for three years. In those three Crawls lucky punters saw young pretenders such as Snow Patrol, Beth Orton and Mogwai take equal billing with legends like Echo and the Bunnymen,

The Wedding Present, Tanya Donnelly and... erm... Moby. For the 10th anniversary of the first Crawl a belated follow-up was organised for 2005, and it was such a success that it's planned to make it a yearly fixture again.

London is filled with unknown bands that deserve your attention. MySpace and music blogs have done a lot to get the music where it belongs, but the Camden Crawl is the best way to experience something fresh and unexpected; and for the price of a wristband, you get to see someone you'd pay an arm and a leg to see anywhere else. And this being Camden the venues are small, cramped and sweaty – pretty bloody perfect then.

CAMDEN CALLING TO THE FARAWAY TOWNS

Just as Samuel Morse was about to succeed in wiring up the USA with telegraph lines to run his famous code, here in the UK two home-grown electrical telegraph pioneers took up a similar undertaking. Charles Wheatstone and Sir William Fothergill Cooke had their own device, based not on the dot-dash-dot model, but rather on a series of needles that turned to certain points on an alphabetical grid when exposed to a burst of electricity along a wire. This meant that no code was needed and, after a breakthrough in sending current over long distances, the pair set out to demonstrate the device.

In 1837, they convinced the London & Birmingham Railway to allow them to lay cables between Camden Town and Euston. The initial demonstrations were so successful that the wires were expanded across other lines, and finally the general public realised the world was suddenly a smaller place. The technology helped to capture John Tawell when, in 1845, he killed his mistress in Slough. Heading for London and freedom, Tawell had no idea how long the arm of the law had grown. News of his crime easily out-raced the train and the police were waiting for him in London, where he was later tried and hanged. The telegraph, for a time, was known as 'the cords that hung John Tawell'.

THERE'S ALWAYS TIME FOR A DRINK
WITHNAIL AND I BEVERAGE CONSUMPTION

9 or so glasses of red wine · 1 half pint of cider

1 shot of lighter fluid (but vinegar will do the trick)

2.5 shots of gin · 6 glasses of sherry

13 glasses of whisky · 1 half pint of ale.

1 gun barrel full of red wine (not filmed)

All of the above goes well with white meat such as kettle stuffed chicken

and a nice side order of Camberwell carrots

A ZED AND TWO NOUGHTS PART 2
GOLDIE

Nothing brings a crowd like the opportunity to see a golden eagle rip the throat out of something. As London Zoo found out when, while its cage was being cleaned, Goldie (a male *Aquila chrysaetos*) took to the skies of London to see what life had to offer beyond the confines of the zoo. Quite a lot as it turned out. Goldie was free as a bird for 12 days back in 1965, and Londoners loved him for it.

As you'd expect, Goldie felt quite at home in Regent's Park but that didn't stop him from making the most of his freedom, with visits to Camden Town, Euston and Tottenham Court Road. Crowds gathered to watch the hapless keepers try to recapture the bird, but despite help from the Fire Brigade and Royal Navy, and state-of-the-art equipment, Goldie was always one flap ahead. Radio 4's John Timpson did his part by trying to lure the bird to ground by playing an Ethiopian bird pipe, much to the delight of audiences, and when Goldie's name was brought up in the House of Commons a great cheer went up. To the eagle this was all blood off a duck's back and he promptly proved his nonchalance by eating one before having a go at a couple of terriers.

All good things come to an end though, and Goldie was finally retrieved (sorry!) after the deputy head keeper tied a dead rabbit to a piece of rope. While the eagle was eating he simply walked up from behind and picked the bird up. The zoo's attendance figures doubled after he was recaptured so you can bet that they kept a tight hold on him...

He escaped again nine months later.

10 THINGS WE WISH WERE TRUE ABOUT CAMDEN

1 The Roundhouse was built by hand by Chuck Norris in 1977. He was so pleased with the building he named his favourite kick after it.

2 Avril Lavigne's 'Sk8er Boi' is based on a real-life Camden punk named Vivian Damage. He's 54 and she broke his heart.

3 Columbo tracked down murderer Oliver Reed to Camden Lock, where he had hidden his murder weapon – a highly polished Doc Martens boot.

4 The waters in the Regent's Canal are said to have mystical healing powers. Jenny Agutter bathed here naked in the 1970s.

5 Tom Baker's Doctor Who bought all his hats from Camden Market. The scarves were knitted back on Gallifrey, though.

6 Legend says that if Jamie Oliver ever eats a slice of £1 pizza from Camden High Street, the monarchy will fall.

7 There is a secret tube station between Camden Town and Chalk Farm known only to Londoners. It's called Golgotha.

8 Tony Blair and Gordon Brown once ran a stall on Camden Market as teenagers. They sold slices of toast – an idea they stole from 'Grange Hill'.

9 Camden is twinned with itself, making it the UK's first conjoined town.

10 The first intercontinental email was sent from here. It read, simply, 'ug x*# shrooms !!!'

Then Susan comes into the room
She's a naughty girl with a lovely smile
Says let's take a drive to Primrose Hill
It's windy there and the view's so nice
London ice can freeze your toes
Like anyone I suppose
I'm holding on for tomorrow.
'For Tomorrow', Blur

THE IDES OF ARCH

With all the destruction that London has suffered over the years you could be forgiven for daydreaming that HG Wells's walking machines really did stomp us underfoot towards the end of the nineteenth century. But Martians turned out to be the least of our worries – what we should have been keeping an eye on was redevelopment.

Take Euston Station (please!) for example. Modern and practical maybe, but also dull and tasteless as dishwater. For a time, though, Euston was the terminus of the mighty London & Birmingham Railway and home to one of the first intercity railway lines ever laid, designed by Robert Stephenson, and the very first railway line to be built into London. Such an achievement needed something grand to house it and the original Euston Station, opened in 1837, was certainly that.

Philip Hardwick and Charles Fox (inventor of the railway switch and designer of Crystal Palace) designed the two-platform station with a 200ft-long engine shed and wrought-iron roof. The station was expanded due to its success and by 1849 a stunning Great Hall (designed by Hardwick's son) complemented the Classical style of the building, whose main focus had always been the 72ft-tall Doric propylaeum at the station's entrance – the Euston Arch.

Inspired by Roman architecture, the arch was charmingly over-the-top even by Victorian standards. For 125 years its granite weathered the elements and survived falling bombs, until 1962 when Progress turned its head, saw the seemingly forever-standing Euston Arch and trampled it underfoot.

The mistakes of the nineteenth century had charming if improbable solutions. When it was discovered that the engines did not have enough power to make the steep crawl up from Euston to Camden, a stationary engine was built within the Roundhouse, from where it hauled the engines via cables.

The mistakes of the 1960s are harder to fix. There was outcry at the time of course, even a campaign headed by then poet laureate Sir John Betjeman to save the arch, but its time had come. One good thing that came out of the destruction of Euston and its arch was that at last conservationists began to recognise such architecture as being just as significant as historical houses and unspoiled landscapes. Many still hold the belief that Euston Arch may one day, phoenix-like, rise from its own rubble, but for now the pieces are scattered far and wide. Its ornamental iron gates are safe at the National Railway Museum in York, while the debris that came from one of London's most recognisable landmarks was used unceremoniously to reinforce the banks of the River Lea.

ISLINGTON
AND CLERKENWELL

ISLINGTON
AND CLERKENWELL

YOU CAN'T BUILD A HOTEL ON A PUB

The Angel, Islington is famous for a few things, but one of its claims to fame is that it's the only public house to have appeared on a Monopoly board.

Originally an inn on the Great North Road (now the corner of Islington High Street and Pentonville Road), The Angel became somewhat of a local landmark and ended up giving its name to the surrounding area. Nowadays it is home to the Islington branch of the Cooperative Bank.

But why's it on the Monopoly board?

Well, during the 1930s the building was home to the Lyons Corner Tea House. Legend has it that, after the games-making company Waddingtons had bought the rights to the American board game, its managing director, Victor Watson, and his secretary stopped off there for a brew and to discuss how they were going to Anglicise the game's street names.

The story goes that they included The Angel to commemorate the event; maybe the biscuits were a little stale that day, as the property occupies the lowly position of the third cheapest on the board.

A few years ago a plaque celebrating the Monopoly connection was erected at the site by Victor Watson's grandson (also called Victor).

ISLINGTONS AROUND THE WORLD

New Islington Millennium Community, Manchester

Islington, Toronto

Islington Hotel, Tasmania

Islington Landing, Virginia

Borough of Islington, Christchurch

Islington, Massachusetts

Suburb of Islington, New South Wales

Islington, Jamaica

DOUGLAS ADAMS AND ISLINGTON

Douglas Adams once said that Islington appeared in his work solely because it meant he could do his research by staring out of the window. The author lived in the area with his wife Jane Belson and their daughter until his move to the US in 1999, so he had plenty of source material.

In *The Hitchhiker's Guide to the Galaxy*, Arthur Dent famously meets the bewitching Trillian at a party in Islington, while the opening lines to *The Hitchhiker*'s sequel, *Life, the Universe and Everything* place the area in a slightly different context: 'The regular early morning yell of horror was the sound of Arthur Dent waking up and suddenly remembering where he was. It wasn't just that the cave was cold, it wasn't just that it was damp and smelly. It was the

fact that the cave was in the middle of Islington and there wasn't a bus due for two million years.'

Other N1 mentions pop up in *Dirk Gently's Holistic Detective Agency* (the eponymous private eye has his office there) and in *So Long, and Thanks for all the Fish,* where Adams tries to capture a little of the spirit of the area: 'A summer's day in Islington, full of the mournful wail of antique-restoring machinery.'

It wasn't until he relocated to Santa Barbara, however, that Adams sat down to pen an ode to his favourite bit of north London in an article entitled 'The Hitchhiker's Guide to Islington' for the *Telegraph* newspaper.

When Adams died in 2001 he was cremated, and his ashes were scattered in Highgate Cemetery.

TWO BARNSBURY LOCALS WHO HAVE NOTHING WHATSOEVER IN COMMON

– Tony Blair lived in Richmond Crescent, while Sir Ian Holm lived in Belitha Villas.

– In *Alien* Ian Holm started out as a good guy but by the end of the movie was revealed to be untrustworthy.
– Tony Blair is the Prime Minister.

– In *The Lord of the Rings* trilogy Ian Holm played a hobbit who couldn't be trusted with the ring of power.
– Tony Blair is a politician.

– In *The Fifth Element* Ian Holm played a religious man who helps a hero to save the world from evil-doers.
– Tony Blair is friends with George W Bush.

– In *A Life Less Ordinary* Ian Holm was stuck in a film that had great potential but was ultimately a let down.
– Tony Blair is New Labour.

– In *The Borrowers* Ian Holm is the leader of a tiny people constantly overshadowed by everything else.
– Tony Blair is the leader of the UK.

– In *Time Bandits* Ian Holm played Napoleon as a leader with an inferiority complex that he overcompensated for.
– Tony Blair says we have to stop now.

That's it, just to let you know the police are still looking for the actor Burt Reynolds, after he stole a dodgem and drove it out of a fairground in Islington. The 59-year-old American eluded capture after a low-speed car chase, and was last seen heading north on the M11 near Saffron Walden.

Chris Morris, wrapping up on one of 'The Day Today' shows

AWESOME WELLS

Sometimes the etymology of a place name is simple. Take Sadler's Wells. Richard Sadler discovered wells on his property in the early 1680s and that's all there is to it really. Sadler was a bit of an opportunist and told anyone who'd listen that his water was the best cure for 'dropsy, jaundice, scurvy, green sickness and other distempers to which females are liable – ulcers, fits of the mother, virgin's fever and hypochondriacal distemper'. This cure-all proved so popular with the well-to-do of London that Sadler set up a 'Musick House' to entertain the visitors.

The music house still thrives today, but you'd be hard pressed to find a bottle of his water in Boots the Chemist. For a time though, the music house looked just as doomed. Ever more unsavoury types found their way there and things slipped into decline with the nadir being a 1699 performance of live cockerel eating by a man billed as The Hibernian Cannibal.

Things of course turned around and in fact the current Sadler's Wells is in its sixth incarnation. It does make you yearn for the good old days though. Who wouldn't like a night out at the theatre complete with the chance to cure a virgin and view a little cock swallowing?

ROCK AND RELIGION

Islington's Gothic-style Union Chapel has to be one of the strangest rock 'n' roll venues in the country. A meeting place for evangelical churchmen and Nonconformists since the seventeenth century, it's probably the last place you'd expect to find a bunch of sweaty indie kids.

In fact, this has to be the only concert venue in the world that regularly saw roadies wiring up speaker stacks in the shadow of a piece of the very same Plymouth rock upon which the *Mayflower* Pilgrim Fathers landed all that time ago.

In late 2004, however, the capital's music lovers were upset to hear that the Chapel was to close its doors to gigs, after local residents' complaints about the noise and a decision to ban alcohol from the main auditorium. In 2006, the venue reopened with a no-alcohol, acoustic-only philosophy.

Of course the Chapel is still a working church and does invaluable work in the local community; its day centre for the homeless has proven very popular, thanks to the better-than-average cooking and the policy of allowing dogs.

On 7 May 2006, Arsenal Football Club played their last competitive game at the Arsenal Stadium, popularly known as Highbury, before relocating a few hundred yards up the road to the spanking-new Emirates Stadium in Ashburton Grove. A sign of the times, the new stadium's name reflects a sponsorship deal, although you can probably forgive the football club for taking the Emirates shilling (to be precise, £100m over 15 years) as the overall cost of the project is put at £390m.

Football, of course, has been awash with money since Rupert Murdoch worked out that the way to jump-start his satellite broadcasting business was to monopolise live football coverage. But Arsenal are no strangers to lavishing huge amounts of money on beautifying stadiums. Having relocated in 1913 from south-east London to the now-abandoned Highbury stadium, designed by the great football stadium architect Archibald Leitch, Arsenal went on a redevelopment spending spree in the 1930s. The West Stand, designed by Claude Waterlow Ferrier and completed in 1932, cost the club

£50,000; in 1935 the famous clock was relocated from the North Stand to the South Stand, as the former gained a roof and the latter gained a new moniker of 'the Clock End'; and the £130,000 East Stand, built to match the West Stand, was inaugurated on 24 October 1936.

The East Stand is a fine monument to the art deco style and houses the famous Marble Halls. Such is its architectural significance, the East Stand is a Grade II listed building, restricting the ability of Arsenal to redevelop it completely, which brings us neatly back to the present day. What used to be a restriction is now a plus point, as the old ground is redeveloped into a collection of residential apartments, 'set within the art deco surroundings of Arsenal Stadium, Highbury', according to the marketing blurb. The North Stand and Clock End, which were completely redeveloped in the relatively recent past to comply with requirements for football stadiums to be all-seater, are being completely redeveloped yet again. The art deco magnificence of the West and East Stands will be retained, at least externally. What this means to fans of art deco architecture, of course, is that what used to be a quasi-public area is now a private residential building.

10 ISLINGTON-RELATED EBAY ITEMS ON SALE RIGHT NOW!*

An engraving of Islington Agricultural Hall – *current bid £00.00*

A copy of *Boxing News* from 1974 covering Islington boxers – *current bid £00.00*

An old amber Islington bottle (JG Webb & Co Ltd) – *current bid £17.05*

A Robert Brothers Circus poster for Islington from the 1970s – *current bid £00.99*

An old railway ticket for Highbury & Islington to Camden Road – *current bid £00.00*

A print of prize dogs at Islington National Show from 1869 – *current bid £4.99*

A genuine antique map of Islington from 1754 – *current bid £00.00*

A despatch note card from Stanmore Springs dated 1953 – *current bid £00.00*

A picture postcard showing Upper Street dated 1907 – *current bid £3.20*

Two tickets to see the Dandy Warhols at the Islington Academy – *current bid £00.01*

* Information correct at time of writing, not reading

> **When a third wave of poverty overwhelmed me, I knew with even greater certitude than when I lived in Clerkenwell that the only complete solution to my problems was suicide.**
>
> Quentin Crisp, *The Naked Civil Servant* (1968)

ISLINGTON'S BENCHES FOR DRUNKS

In 2004, Islington Council decided that it was time to do something about the drunks littering its streets: make them more comfortable.

As part of a £1m regeneration scheme, the council employed a swanky architectural firm to design a special set of benches that could easily accommodate up to 10 hardcore fans of strong brew. The designers conducted an incredibly thorough analysis of the area, including discovering which specific tree branches are favoured by defecating pigeons. They then thoughtfully designed their benches so that they lean in towards the back support, as this is apparently the best position for adult drinkers (although lying down also seems popular).

The benches also included handy ashtrays, rubbish bins and a low wall for privacy.

1067 AND BEYOND

Islington is important. No, seriously. It may not be the first stop on any London visitor's itinerary – hell, even the Germans bombed it as an afterthought (once they'd levelled vast sections of central London and were heading back home they dumped any bombs they still had right here). But nevertheless, 40 Northampton Road is one of the most interesting addresses in London because of what is stored there: the London Metropolitan Archives (LMA).

Don't take our word for it; the Museums, Libraries and Archive Council designates the collection as one of national and international importance. Some 45 miles of information dating from 1067 is stored here in strongrooms, and anything with a strongroom has got to be worth a visit. The array of material on offer is staggering. It covers architecture (from pigeon lofts to Tower Bridge); medicine (including archives from 130 hospitals); education; transport; law and order; migration; science and technology; religion (archives from more than 800 churches); customs; and campaigning activities (loads of information on the Gordon Riots, female suffrage and anti-apartheid protests).

It's not simply a place for dumping records though, oh no. The material is used to reveal even more about how London used to be in order to provide insight into how we can make the capital a better place to live in now. Among the special projects that the LMA carry out are detailed overviews on subjects such as how London was governed between 1538 and 1965, and a thorough history of black and Asian Londoners dating back to 1536 (showing that London's multicultural heritage goes back a lot further than many assume).

And then there are the maps – if you have a thing for cartography then bring a sleeping bag. The printed maps date back to the sixteenth century and include a thematic series showing such details as bomb damage. On top of that, more than 250,000 prints, watercolours, etchings and photographs should keep you busy for an afternoon.

The Archives are totally free to visit and use, and are open most days. There's even a free enquiry service about what records are held, but there is a charge for copying the material. There is also a family history research service, making it the place to aim for if you want to find out why that distant relative of yours ended up with his head on a spike. Alternatively, if you always figured you had a book on London in you somewhere then take a laptop, some sandwiches and change for the coffee machine, as the archive has literally centuries of starting points. Just don't write *The Da Vinci Code II*.

Arthur wandered in a blissed-out haze and looked at all the shops which, in Islington, are quite a useful bunch, as anyone who regularly needs old woodworking tools, Boer War helmets, drag, office furniture or fish will readily confirm.

Douglas Adams, *So Long, and Thanks For All the Fish* (1984)

Canonbury Tower, one of the oldest buildings in Islington, has had quite an eventful history over the years. It was built in the early 1500s by William Bolton (the Master of Works for the chapel in Westminster Abbey) when he fancied something with a view. As bad luck would have it he died the same year it was finished. A couple of years later and Thomas Cromwell had moved in. From here he organised the proper dissolution of monasteries on behalf of Henry VIII. The King made £900,000 out of that historical gazumping and Cromwell was rewarded with Canonbury Manor. That must have seemed like a good deal to Cromwell right up until Henry had him executed only a year later and used the Manor's money to pay his divorce settlement to Anne of Cleves.

John Dudley ('the bear of Warwick'!) had the place for a while, but then he, too, was executed. Sir John Spencer, Lord Mayor of London, took charge of the place in 1570 and it was his daughter, Elizabeth, who eloped with the Earl of Northampton. He disguised himself as a baker's boy and smuggled his (diminutive, we presume) love out in a baker's basket. After Spencer died the couple inherited everything. The Tower is still owned by the family although over the years it has been leased out to the likes of Francis Bacon (the statesman and philosopher) and Washington Irving, and it developed a strong connection with the Masons which continues to this day. The Tower is currently home to the Canonbury Masonic Research Centre.

FIVE FILMS MADE BY GAINSBOROUGH STUDIOS

The Lodger: A Story of the London Fog (1926) – Hitchcock starts his love affair with the thriller.

Oh, Mr Porter (1937) – Will Hay in a classic comedy penned by Val (*The Day the Earth Caught Fire*) Guest.

Millions Like Us (1943) – Women do their bit for the war effort in an aircraft factory during World War II.

Fanny by Gaslight (1944) – banned in the US years before they worked out what a fanny was.

The Wicked Lady (1945) – Margaret Lockwood out-swashes James Mason's buckle as a highwaywoman.

THE GRANITA PACT

From its bare wooden tabletops to its overpriced starters, in the mid-1990s the Granita restaurant at 127 Upper Street was the very epitome of the stark trendiness that typified the era. It was also a favourite destination of Tony Blair, when in 1994, he supposedly invited his friend Gordon there to talk about the future of the Labour Party after the death of John Smith.

There is no concrete evidence to suggest a formal deal was ever made at Granita or anywhere else, although *The Guardian* newspaper did uncover a note in 2003, which seemed to suggest a leadership agreement of some sort had been made. Granita closed down in 2003, in the same week that Channel 4 aired a dramatisation of the Granita story. Now at 127 Upper Street you'll find the Desperados Mexican eatery. The owners assure us the name is in no way a comment on the current state of the Labour Party.

HOLLYWOOD BY THE CANAL

If on your wanderings through Islington you stumble across Poole Street near Regent's Canal, you'd be sure to spot the old Gainsborough Studios. Even after their conversion into loft apartments there's something grand about the buildings. A clue to what went on inside is found in the courtyard – an enormous sculpted head with more than a passing resemblance to Alfred Hitchcock.

This was the site of Gainsborough Studios – a name the refurbished complex has retained – where Hitchcock learned his trade (*see box, left*). It started life as a power station, but lay disused after World War I. It became Islington Studios in 1919 and home to a US film company, the Famous Players-Lasky, before being sold in 1924 to Michael Balcon, who remade it as Gainsborough Studios. The company's logo was based on a portrait of the actress Sarah Siddons by Thomas Gainsborough.

Hitchcock was far from the only personality to work there. Will Hay, Margaret Lockwood, James Mason, Stewart Granger and Boris Karloff were just some of the stars who made films at Gainsborough Studios. World War II closed the studios once more, and despite a brief resurgence as a Rank studio after the war, its film-making days were pretty much over.

After years standing empty and brief employment as a warehouse, the studios became a bingo hall and resurfaced in their present form. The glory days are long over, but it's a small comfort to know that there is a film studio and editing suite within the buildings, ensuring that celluloid continues to flicker somewhere within its heart.

10 ISLINGTON-BASED COP SHOWS WE'D LIKE TO SEE, STARRING FAMOUS RESIDENTS

Bacon & Eggs – The ghost of Sir Francis Bacon teams up with a maverick detective called Eggs.

Halley's Comets – Edmund Halley sets up a team of government-sanctioned crime-fighting astronomers.

Hogarth Brooks – The artist William Hogarth goes undercover among the Islington line-dancing community.

Red Raleigh Racer – Sir Walter Raleigh is found frozen but still alive and becomes a cycle cop in his old neighbourhood.

Waugh: What Is It Good For? – Evelyn Waugh returns home from the Vietnam War and finds his jungle-fighting skills essential as a bobby.

Orwell That Ends Well – George Orwell has a change of heart and now works for a totalitarian Islington police force.

Lamb Chops – Charles Lamb, author and karate master, fights crime with his bare hands.

Hornby's Railway – Nick Hornby is a burned-out British Transport Police Cop.

Lenin & McCartney – Time-travelling cop on the edge, Vladimir Ulyanov Lenin, is partnered with a talking Volkswagen Beetle.

Monopoly of Crime – the board game predicts bank robberies. Before they happen!

LITTLE EGYPT IN LITTLE-KNOWN SUBURB

Flanked by the mildly hostile Caledonian Road and the tired razzmatazz of Upper Street, Barnsbury is one of those peculiar London areas that seemingly slip through the capital's cognisance.

At its heart, spiritual, geographical and architectural, is Cloudesley Square and its centrally placed Holy Trinity Church. This imposing building, based on King's College, Cambridge, was designed by Charles Barry, architect of the Houses of Parliament.

But the real unexpected gem is Richmond Avenue, home of a startling bit of architecture ignored by every guidebook. Barnsbury becomes Little Egypt, as you pass a long terrace of houses embellished with dog-sized sphinxes and sleek obelisks bearing the word 'Nile'. Round the corner there's a real villagey atmosphere, with parks and trees and some of north London's most charming boozers (with good old patriotic names like the Crown and the Albion).

SCRATCHING FANNY OF COCK LANE

These days the only real entertainment that Cock Lane can offer is to giggling schoolboys who delight in its entendre-laden name. But back in 1760, the street was home to the capital's most famous spectre known as (and we swear we're not making this up) Scratching Fanny.

To cut a long (and possibly prurient) story short, the legend of Cock Lane began when William Kent took up lodgings at number 33 along with Fanny, the sister of his recently demised wife. Kent then lent his new landlord, Bill Parsons, a substantial amount of money that Bill didn't seem too keen to pay back.

One day, while Kent was away on business overnight, Fanny asked Parsons' 11-year-old daughter, Elizabeth, to sleep alongside her, and it was then that she heard strange knocking and scratching noises in the middle of the night.

Instead of just blaming the plumbing, Fanny insisted that the rattlings were a message from her dead sister informing her that she would soon be punished for her misdeeds. Sure enough, despite a swift relocation away from Cock Lane, Fanny died shortly afterwards from smallpox.

Meanwhile, Parsons (who still owed money to his former lodger) was claiming that the rattlings at Cock Lane had continued, and were now saying that Kent had actually murdered his wife with arsenic. The ghost promptly became a citywide celebrity and soon people were paying to hear the ghost, which seemed to be most active when young Elizabeth was around.

Finally the ghost declared that it would prove its authenticity if Kent would spend a night next to Fanny's coffin in the crypt of St John's Church, Clerkenwell. Kent obliged and was accompanied by a gang of 'eminent men' including Dr Samuel Johnson, who really should have known better.

The men kept their ghastly vigil until dawn but no knocking, scratching, bells or whistles were heard and the ghost was declared a fraud. Shortly afterwards young Elizabeth was put under secret surveillance and it was soon discovered what Mulder and Scully could have told you within five minutes: little Lizzy had a piece of wood hidden in her pants and would knock on it to create the ghostly effect.

And so ends the tale of Scratching Fanny of Cock Lane.

THE CITY

THE CITY

WHERE IS LONDON? Only the dimmest of dim tourists could make such a dimishly dim enquiry, right? Not so. They'd deserve to receive a pat on the backpack and a ceremonial tin opener as a prize for opening such an unexpectedly pedantic can of worms. Our city's name is impossible to pin down to any official boundary. It's not even one city. Nor even is it the officially confirmed capital of the UK (or England or Britain or... what a terribly confused land we live in). All we can say with any certainty is that London is the largest non-existent place on Earth.

'So what's that big grey noisy thing outside my window?', you might ask. What we tend to think of as London actually comprises two tiny cities and several valleys-worth of boroughs. Altogether, this administrative mélange is called 'Greater London'. So you might expect the inner parts, the kernel at the heart of this messy conglomerate, to be called, simply, London. But it's not. At least not any longer. The most ancient, Roman part, which was once called London, is now officially known as 'the City', or 'the City of London'. But never just 'London'. And then the other great atrium at the heart of 'London', the bit the tourists tend to flock to, is known as 'the City of Westminster'. London itself seems to have wriggled through the cracks like a weasel in a mixed metaphor.

So 'London' is really just a convenient tag for something too organic and random to be carefully defined. It works well, though. 'Cities of London and Westminster plus Surrounding Boroughs Calling' by The Clash just wouldn't scan.

THE FIVE MOST WORDY LIVERY COMPANIES

1. The Worshipful Company of Tobacco Pipe Makers and Tobacco Blenders
2. The Worshipful Company of Coachmakers and Coach Harness Makers
3. The Worshipful Company of Chartered Secretaries and Administrators
4. The Worshipful Company of Tin Plate Workers alias Wire Workers
5. The Worshipful Company of Gold and Silver Wyre Drawers

If you seek my monument, look around... If you seek the finest offices in the City, look no further: 9,660 square metres, high specification.

Crass allusion to Wren's epitaph by the developers of Paternoster Square

HOW TO ROB THE BANK OF ENGLAND AND MAKE GOOD YOUR ESCAPE

Well, we're not telling you how to do the first bit; that would be irresponsible. But here's how to make your way to the river without being seen. (Like any good villain, you're going to use a speedboat to escape.)

First, head down into Bank tube station. This place is so busy you can easily lose any pursuer in the crowds. Better yet, a preposterously long set of tunnels and escalators will take you to Monument station – already halfway to the river.

Emerge, once again, to the world above. Head through the crowds of confused tourists below the Monument ('Is this Nelson's Column?') and head up Pudding Lane. A first right should

take you into the solitude of St George's Lane. That's the hard bit done – a series of lonely alleys and little-known snickleways now guarantees furtive progress. Take the twisting Botolph Alley followed by St Dunstan's Lane. Pass through the bombed-out churchyard and on into St Dunstan's Hill. A quick sprint down the slope of Cross Lane should then take you to the riverfront.

Your getaway boat is waiting a little to the east at the Tower Millennium Pier. But it's a set-up. Your accomplice has picked a parking spot equidistant from HM Customs, the armed guards of the Tower, and the 6-inch guns of HMS *Belfast*. Better luck next time.

UPS AND DOWNS IN THE CITY

The City might be covered in roads and buildings and about as verdant as an oil rig, but if you're savvy, and take the time, you can still trace the ancient topography of this land. We're talking a couple of millennia, here. Before the Romans came along with their civilisation nonsense, and turned the British tribes into the first nimbys. 'They're going to build an Olympic-sized amphitheatre behind my wattle-and-daub hut? Bugger that! I'm not paying my taxes just so a couple of muscle-brained gladiators can grapple in my backyard.'

Yes, before the Italians invented London, the area really was just fields and hills and streams. And it still is, underneath its civic clothing of concrete, glass and tarmac. The best way to appreciate all this is to get on a bike. The ups and downs of hills and valleys become much more apparent that way.

One great example: the River Fleet valley. This steep-sided trench bisects the City and Holborn. Thousands of people cross this great divide every day. And most have no idea that they're passing over an ancient river bed. You can still just about see the river today, or at least its outflow, if you peer over the edge of Blackfriars Bridge during low tide. Alternatively, you can get a job in the sewers, for the buried Fleet now serves as a storm-relief drain. But even if you can't catch a glimpse of the water, you can

clearly see its effects. Farringdon Road, which follows the course of the river, is flanked by a series of climbing side streets. These were once the banks of the Fleet, and still bear telling names such as Turnmill Street and, indeed, Fleet Street.

Although this stretch of the Fleet has been covered over for many centuries, there's no denying its presence can still be felt. Empty, dusty buildings. The absence of people. Few food outlets. Germs everywhere. You can feel the malaise, you can breathe the history. And it's not nice.

At a right angle to the Fleet, the mighty Thames, though embanked and squashed, still flows along its Neolithic route. The sloping streets of the north bank are testament to millennia of erosion by the great river. Garlick Hill, Fish Street Hill, Addle Hill. There are at least 10 such names between the level of Cannon Street and the Thames.

Biggest of all is Ludgate Hill, home of St Paul's Cathedral. Then, further east, stands Cornhill. This high ground has always been a focal point for great buildings, from the giant Roman forum to the modern-day financial institutions. It's humbling to think that these very mounds and dips were causing sore feet and traffic problems 70 generations ago. The shape of modern London and the locations of its great buildings are intimately tied to the same geography that made London such an attractive place to settle in the first place.

ABRIDGED AND INACCURATE HISTORY OF THE CITY OF LONDON, TOLD THROUGH THE FORGOTTEN AND FRANKLY RUBBISH MEDIUM OF THE CLERIHEW

Roman Emperor, Claudius Caesar
Not all that bad, but a bit of a teaser
He founded and fitted Londinium town
Then taunted the Britons 'Why come, burn it down'

***

Thrice-Mayor Dick Whittington
Got lots of shitting done
T'was the reason, we're told
He left the streets paved with gold

***

Sir Christopher Wren
Did not build Big Ben
But marshalled his peoples
To construct tall steeples

***

Lords Rogers and Foster
Said 'Oh, it'll cost-yer'
But make the right deal
And we'll build glass and steel

TOP 10 TALL BUILDINGS

2006	2012
1. Tower 42 – 600ft	1. Bishopsgate Tower – 945ft
2. 30 St Mary Axe – 590ft	2. Heron Tower – 794ft
3. CityPoint – 417ft	3. Leadenhall Building – 738ft
4. Shakespeare Tower – 403ft	4. 20 Fenchurch Street – 629ft
4.= Lauderdale Tower – 403ft	5. Tower 42 – 600ft
4.= Cromwell Tower – 403ft	6. St Mary Axe – 590ft
7. St Helen's – 387ft	7. Broadgate Tower – 538ft
8. 99 Bishopsgate – 341ft	8. 100 Middlesex Street – 440ft
9. Drapers Gardens – 328ft	9. CityPoint – 417ft
10. Lloyd's Building – 312ft	10. Willis Building – 410ft

(Source: SkyscraperPage.com, May 2006)

ALIGNING THE MARKETS

Mysterious 'ley lines' are said to criss-cross the ancient topography of London. Some have suggested that the locations of places of antiquity, such as churches, form mystical chains of energy. Well, how's the following for a crackpot theory? Tower 42, or the NatWest Tower as it's more commonly known, is the centre of a nexus of numinous power.

Come again?

It's well known that, when viewed from above, the tower's plan resembles the logo of NatWest Bank. So the architect, Richard Seifert, has clearly built symbolism into the design. But did he go one step further? Look again at a plan view of the tower. If you draw lines from its centre, extending outwards through the three shortest edges, there is something of a coincidence.

Each of the three lines points directly at one of London's ancient markets. To the south, the line extends through Leadenhall to Old Billingsgate; to the north-east, it passes through Spitalfields; and to the north-west, the target is Smithfield meat market. It's as though a message is intended: in the modern city, it is the financial markets that are of central importance.

LONDON AS A RUSSIAN DOLL

London is not just eccentric, it's also concentric. The various walls, barriers and boundaries that surround it can be compared to Dante's circles of Hell, or the growth rings of a tree, depending on your psyche.

At the core is the circular hub of Bank station, from which thousands of eager workers spill each morning. This mirrors the fortress-like curtain wall surrounding the Bank of England, which gives the station its name. Further out, the 'square mile' is enclosed by the crumbling remains of the Roman and medieval city walls – best viewed on Tower Hill and south of the Barbican.

Then there's the somewhat intangible 'ring of steel', a security perimeter set up in the early 1990s after a series of IRA bombs. A little bit further and we come to where a wall of fortifications once surrounded London as an untested Civil War defence.

Finally, there are the modern ovals, etched into the map during the age of mass transport and rapid communication. The inner ring road, the Congestion Zone, the Circle line, tube zones 1 through 6, telephone codes 020 7 and 020 8, post codes EC1 to WC1. And, greatest of all, the M25 orbital that defines the ultimate limits of the capital.

No wonder Londoners often have a sense of feeling trapped.

FROM GORDON RIOTS TO GORDON BROWN There's a building site on Farringdon Street that you really should pay attention to. Well, it'll probably be a glass and steel office complex by the time you read this, but track it down anyway.

Number 14, about halfway between the Holborn Viaduct and Ludgate Circus, has had more than its fair share of history. If we head back to the days of jousting and wenches, the site was occupied by the notorious Fleet Prison. This benighted jail was destroyed on four occasions – by revolting peasants, by the Great Fire, by Gordon rioters and by the Corporation of the City of London, who finally did away with it in 1846.

Its next incarnation was the Congregational Memorial Hall. In 1900, a jamboree of like-minded lefties gathered here to discuss ways of making life fairer for the common man. Somewhere deep in the meeting's minutes lies the beginnings of the Labour Party. And so the governing body we know and deride today was inauspiciously founded above the ruins of a medieval prison.

Since then, a couple of office developments have disgraced the site. Let's hope the next iteration lives up to its heritage.

On film, at least, Londoners get: MOSTLY EATEN
- to spot Alfred Hitchcock in *Blackmail* (1929)
- baked by the sun in *The Day the Earth Caught Fire* (1961)
- attacked by pigeons in *The Core* (2003)
- wet (and eaten) by a monster in *Split Second* (1992)
- infected by angry monkeys in *28 Days Later* (2002)
- sucked by space vampires in *Lifeforce* (1985)
- blown up by a terrorist in *Night Hawks* (1981)
- harvested by aliens in *The Quatermass Conclusion* (1979)
- eaten by cannibals in *Death Line* (1972)
- mauled (and eaten) by a lycanthrope in *An American Werewolf in London* (1981)
- cursed by demons in *Night of the Demon* (1957)
- barbecued (and eaten) by dragons in *Reign of Fire* (2002)
- filmed by a killer camera in *Peeping Tom* (1960)
- bitten by a snake in *Venom* (1982)
- bitten (and eaten) by zombies in *Shaun of the Dead* (2004)
- serial killed by Richard Attenborough in *10 Rillington Place* (1971)
- strangled by kipper ties in *Frenzy* (1972)
- sung to by The Beatles in *A Hard Day's Night* (1964)
- shagged (and probably eaten) by Michael Caine in *Alfie* (1966)

A PARK OF UNUSUAL DEATHS

No guidebook on quirky London could possibly be complete without a brief mention of Postman's Park. Not only does this place have a silly name (from its one-time proximity to the GPO), but it also has a unique accoutrement: a wall of unusual deaths.

Tucked away in a little sheltered area are 47 ceramic plaques commemorating Victorians who expired in heroic and emotively phrased ways. Take, for instance, Sarah Smith, 'pantomime artiste'. She met her end in 1863 'of terrible injuries received when attempting in her inflammable dress to extinguish the flames which had enveloped her companion'. And William Donald, who was 'drowned in the Lea trying to save a lad from a dangerous entanglement of weed'.

You just don't get dangerous entanglements of weed any more. Not outside of Brixton, anyhow.

Saddest of all must be David Selves who, in 1886, 'supported his drowning playfellow and sank with him clasped in his arms'.

Stirring stuff, and it's a pity this tradition of commemorating extraordinary ordinary folk hasn't persisted. Though it would probably have to involve Esther Rantzen these days, and nobody wants that.

> **Aged marshals, grey, dreary ladies, decadent Marlboroughs and Churchills. It was a dying congregation gathered there and I am afraid the Labour Cabinet didn't look too distinguished either. It felt like the end of an epoch, possibly even the end of a nation.**
>
> Churchill's funeral at St Paul's, as described by Richard Crossman in *The Crossman Diaries 1964-1970*

FIVE REAL CITY CHURCHES WITH SILLY NAMES

All Hallows Staining

St Andrew-by-the-wardrobe

St Margaret Pattens

St Vedast-alias-Foster

St Sepulchre-without-Newgate

LOST
IN THE BARBICAN

The Barbican isn't everyone's cuppa. The enigmatic 1970s concrete village and 'arts complex' is one giant sprawling bastard of saw-tooth towers, windswept causeways and gloopy, Fairy-Liquid ponds. Here, the streets aren't paved with gold, but with endless yellow lines that describe entirely notional walking routes. On first impression, it seems as if the whole shebang was put together via some elaborate game of pin-the-tail-on-the-donkey.

It's rare to find a description of the Barbican that doesn't contain the word 'labyrinthine'. With good reason. The trials of Theseus, trapped in the maze of Knossos, are nothing compared with a stroll around here. There's even a sculpture of a minotaur to encourage the allusion. Why is it designed like this? Presumably to provide an exhilarating uncertainty for the residents: that they might not actually be able to find their own homes.

And who exactly are these inhabitants? There must be hundreds of apartments in the complex, which includes three of the tallest tower blocks in the country. But there's never any bugger there. Except the occasional and very confused delivery person. Rumour has it that errant postal workers threatened with disciplinary action don't get the sack, as the jokes would have us believe. No. They get a month's worth of deliveries to the Barbican.

GETTING ON YOUR HIGH HORSE

As the old saying goes: 'You can lead a horse to the top of a public building, but you can't make it jump.' Well, something like that.

The City certainly has a history of equine elevation. In 1600, a Scottish fellow named Banks led his special dancing horse, called Morocco, to the top of the old St Paul's Cathedral, where it pranced about on the roof a bit and attracted huge crowds. Splendid.

Those crazy City types. What will they do next?

Well, the same again, apparently. A couple of centuries later, in 1818, somebody repeated the trick. On the Monument. With a pony, this time. Again, large numbers turned out to see the spectacle. The things they had to do for entertainment before TV was invented.

Who knows why these things happen? London has an infinite capacity for random, madcap displays of the unexpected. Next thing we know, they'll be parading a 40-ton, mechanical, time-travelling elephant down the Mall.

What?

Oh.

OK, I'M GETTING HUNGRY NOW

The City of London is replete with foody streets; the last echoes of erstwhile trading precincts. But how appropriate are they today? Well, there's not so much as a crumb on Oat Lane, to the north of St Paul's Cathedral; it is now just a service road. Likewise Milk Street — more dreary than dairy. Greater success on nearby Honey Lane, where the City Tavern offers a glazed salad that may or may not feature honey. But, then, it's officially on Lawrence Lane (whoever he is), so it wouldn't count anyhow.

Pressing on south, it's a relief to find some nominative resonance at last, in the form of the bap selection in Chez Gerard (on Bread Street). And several eateries along Garlick Hill offer the eponymous flavouring in their dishes. But then it all goes wrong along Poultry, with ne'er a whiff of clucking foul.

Cornhill offers dubious pickings, in the form of gastropub corn chips. Likewise, Lime Street's titular fulfilment can only be assuaged with the ice 'n' slice of a g&t. And it's a mighty relief to find no puddings on Pudding Lane. The infamous origin of the Great Fire was actually named after the entrail leftovers of the butcher's trade, which were colloquially referred to as puddings.

But after a mostly fruitless search, literally, a satisfying cod and chips on Fish Street Hill made everything seem right with the world.

ST DUNSTAN-IN-THE-EAST

The City is peppered with hidden churches. Many of them by Christopher Wren. Many of them scarred victims of World War II. But none are as hidden, as Wrenish or as scarred as St Dunstan-in-the-East.

St Dunstan's is the textbook example of an oasis of calm in an ocean of frenzy. Only metres from the roar of Great Tower Street, the secret garden at its heart seems hermetically sealed from the surrounding activity.

The complicated yet elegant Gothic spire is Wren at his finest, pre-empting the design of *Thunderbird 3* by some 300 years. The rest of the church dates from the 1820s. An unfortunate encounter with the Luftwaffe has left only a shell of the once-grand nave. But the words 'cloud', 'silver' and 'lining' spring to mind, when you see how an act of aggression led to such a peaceful open space.

A knee-high fountain idly bubbles within a ring of benches. Climbing ivy colours the ruined nave and tower. And stone archways leading back to the flawed world outside are artfully hidden round corners to maintain the illusion of Eden.

FINDING THE CENTRE OF THE CITY

In something as confusingly laid out as the City, it's helpful to have some bearings. A good start, as with any maze, is to find the centre.

Here's one way to do it. Print out a map of the City and paste it onto card. After carefully cutting around the outline, try balancing the map on a pin head. Got it cracked? If so, congratulations, you've literally pinpointed the centre of gravity for the 'square mile'.

The point should lie on King Street, just north of Cheapside. Interestingly, this is exactly halfway between Ludgate Hill and Cornhill, twin mounds of ancient significance. Spooky, huh?

More traditionally, the heart of the City is London Stone, on Cannon Street. This mysterious and ancient clump of limestone has been part of London myth since ancient times, and the Romans are said to have measured all distances in Britain from this point. Whatever its romantic origins (and many have been offered) London Stone is today set in a pathetically anonymous grilled window in the former offices of a banking corporation (though, at the time of writing, there are plans to demolish this building and improve the stone's visibility). It might be the centre of town, but it's no longer the centre of attention.

HOW TO VISIT CAMBRIDGESHIRE IN YOUR LUNCH HOUR

Ely Place has a bit of an identity crisis. It hugs the boundary between the City and Camden borough, but thumbs its nose at both. This gated, private road is the jurisdiction of neither the Met nor the City constabulary; so, in theory, anyone entering the street is immune from arrest. Given the 'current climate of increased security', however, please don't put this to the test.

Ely Place forms part of the estates that once belonged to the bishops of Ely. Some sources claim that this technically makes it an enclave of Cambridgeshire, though nobody seems to know exactly what this means. Whatever, this is certainly a place of charm. If you're extremely lucky, so the guidebooks tell us, you'll be greeted by besuited Beadles guarding the entrance. They must exist, but we've yet to encounter one.

Another hide-and-seek facet of Ely Place is its pub, the Olde Mitre Tavern. Now this definitely does exist, but takes some finding. Head down a near-invisible alleyway next to the ancient St Etheldreda's church, and it's there on your right. This is an ancient and historic place, and counts Elizabeth I as one of its former patrons. Nowadays, it's full of jewellers from Hatton Garden. The Olde Mitre is, to use the cliché, a hidden gem, as precious as anything they might turn their hands to.

THE SOUTH BANK

THE SOUTH BANK

GRAB, SLIDE AND GRIND

If you want an example of the laid-back nature of the South Bank compared to, say, the Square Mile then all you have to do is try to pull a frontside lipslide and see what happens. Unless you're pretty good on a skateboard you'll probably end up eating concrete, but while on the South Bank you may get helped to your feet and encouraged to give it another go, in the City all you can expect is a £20 on-the-spot fine and maybe an ASBO.

The Queen Elizabeth Hall Undercroft has been the focus point for skateboarding in the UK since the 1970s and while many of the original skaters are more likely to pull a muscle than an ollie, the tradition is still ongoing and accepted as part of the South Bank's diverse cultural mix.

In fact the South Bank has done more than simply accept the skateboarders, it has actively encouraged and even provided for them over the years. In 2004 'skateable sculptures' arrived outside the Queen Elizabeth Hall and a permanent graffiti-friendly backdrop was installed – the space here being perhaps even more earnestly defended than skating space on the steps each weekend.

SOUTH BANK RANDOM FACTS

- The new City Hall building was constructed like a giant jigsaw puzzle. Every single panel is slightly different.

- The South Bank Lion overlooking Westminster Bridge was the original figurehead for the Red Lion Brewery.

- The Pool of London, the wide section of the Thames just upstream of Tower Bridge, was once known as 'London's Larder' and 'The Breakfast Table of London' as the majority of London's food was delivered and stored there.

- Butlers Wharf has the largest group of Victorian warehouses left in London.

- The Imperial War Museum was previously home to St Mary of Bethlehem Royal Hospital, better known as Bedlam Insane Asylum.

- The Scoop, an 800-seat open-air amphitheatre outside City Hall, has a sunken terrace for seating based on the interior spiral ramp that runs up inside its egg-shaped neighbour.

> **It's a piece of complete tat really.**
> Iain Sinclair talking to Londonist.com about the London Eye (2005)

NOT A FERRIS WHEEL

Londoners seem as proud of the London Eye as they are baffled by the Millennium Dome, but most of us do our favourite erection a great disservice by calling it simply a Ferris wheel. It is in fact an 'observation wheel'. What's the bloody difference you may well ask, to which the reply would be, you can't rock your average London Eye 'pod' or hang out of the top spitting overpriced soft drinks at the people below. Also, Ferris wheels rely on gravity to keep their cars level, while an Eye pod is all about the mechanics. Our Eye is also held in place by a single A-frame, while a more traditional fairground ride uses the same old-fashioned frame that holds your bicycle wheels in place.

Since the success of the London Eye a number of other cities have jumped on our bandwagon, resulting in a clamour to get bigger and better observation wheels up in their own skylines. These include Las Vegas, Melbourne, Moscow, Shanghai, Singapore and, erm... Birmingham.

DRINK UP ME HEARTIES YO HO!

Given the choice, any self respecting pirate would rather yo ho ho it in the Caribbean instead of sludging around the murky waters of the Thames, but London once had quite a role to play in the history of piracy.

Until 1700, all cases of piracy involving British subjects or colonies had to be heard in London, making Marshalsea prison in Borough the one place that no privateer would want to find himself. A single wall still stands just off Borough High Street but it's more remarked upon these days in connection with Charles Dickens, whose father was also held there.

Arrival at Marshalsea was followed by a swift trial and most were sentenced to death at Execution Dock – itself only a mile or so down from Tower Bridge at Wapping. A pirate execution caused quite a stir with Londoners, who would join in the procession, while boats gathered along the river so its occupants could hear the sentenced men's last words. The condemned were hanged at low tide and then left until the Thames had washed over the bodies three times. Corpses were then preserved in tar before finally being hung inside a gibbet, where the bodies would remain as a warning to others.

Executioner's Dock is long gone, but the Captain Kidd pub overlooks the site, named after William Kidd who was strung up there twice – the rope snapped the first time.

Though many ended their days here, London also gave birth to more than a few pirates, including the cross-dressing Mary Read and Captain Edward Low. Low was known to torture captured crews, forcing them to eat their own-sliced off body parts before killing them.

The Thames itself was also a source of temptation when London Bridge offered the only route across the river. The city relied on the Thames as its supply line so it was only a matter of time before home-grown pirates tried their hand at re-routing the cargo. Thieves would board ships and commandeer the goods, or wait until dark, cutting lines and following drifting craft until they hit the bank somewhere downstream.

More securely moored is the *Golden Hinde* at Pickford Wharf. Francis Drake may have sailed the galleon with the blessing of Queen Elizabeth I, but to the Spanish he was a pirate through and through, making a tour of the Hinde unmissable for Jack Sparrow fans.

A SLICE OF SLOVENIA IN SE1
Bermondsey Street is situated in one of those up and coming neighbourhoods where home-owners drop a *lot* of money for the postcode, so it takes a little extra effort to stand out from the crowd, especially if your little slice of SE1 is tucked away in Carmarthen Place. Full marks then to whoever had the idea of shipping across a state-of-the-art prefab from Slovenia. That's going one better than a 'Billy' shelving unit from IKEA.

The building is constructed from solid timber sourced from a sustainable forest in Siberia while the foundations are specially laid so as not to harm the surrounding area. It now seems not at all out of place tucked in behind the main street, itself made up of mostly listed buildings. When completed the curved building will be stained black thereby helping to restore the heritage of black timber houses in the area.

You've picked the wrong town to be hung in, Mr Blaine.
The Sunday Times in reference to David Blaine's much-derided 'Above the Below' endurance stunt in which he was suspended 30 feet in the air in a transparent Plexiglas sealed case for 44 days over the south bank of the Thames in 2003.

LONDON'S ROOMS

City Hall's top deck is lovingly referred to as London's Living Room, which begs the question where all the other rooms are located...

Westminster makes for an ideal bedroom, just ask your local MP. Don't worry, you'll soon get used to the sound of the tourists spinning in their wheel.

Brick Lane is the kitchen, but someone's moved the table and chair from the Hampstead Heath dining room.

Nappy Valley around Clapham Junction is the kid's room – can't get in there for pushchairs at the moment.

Croydon is the smallest room in the house. Second door on your left, but be careful because the light doesn't work.

The spare room has to be the white elephant formerly knows as the **Dome**. It's the one room no one ever knows what to do with and tends to fill up with junk.

LONDON MAYOR KEN LIVINGSTONE
in his own words

- *If Voting Changed Anything, They'd Abolish It* (the title of his autobiography)

- Worldwide capitalism kills more people every day than Hitler did. And he was crazy.

- When you see someone trying to manoeuvre [a 4x4] round the school gates you have to think, you are a complete idiot.

- Anybody who enjoys being in the House of Commons probably needs psychiatric help.

- What a squalid and irresponsible little profession it is. Nothing prepares you for how bad Fleet Street really is until it craps on you from a great height.

- You can't expect to work for the Daily Mail Group and have the rest of society treat you with respect as a useful member of society, because you are not.

- I would have thought that for the organisers of the Tour de France, the benefit of coming to London is having famous sites in the background as the cyclists whiz past.

- George Bush is just about everything that is repellent in politics... I look forward to [him] being overthrown as much as I looked forward to Saddam Hussein being overthrown.

- In this city 300 languages are spoken and the people that speak them live side by side in harmony. This city typifies what I believe is the future of the human race and a future where we grow together and we share and we learn from each other.

- Only some ghastly dehumanised moron would want to get rid of the Routemaster.

- In the days that follow look at our airports, look at our sea ports and look at our railway stations, and even after your cowardly attack, you will see that people from the rest of Britain, people from around the world will arrive in London to become Londoners and to fulfil their dreams and achieve their potential. They choose to come to London, as so many have come before because they come to be free, they come to live the life they choose, they come to be able to be themselves. They flee you because you tell them how they should live. They don't want that and nothing you do, however many of us you kill, will stop that flight to our city where freedom is strong and where people can live in harmony with one another. Whatever you do, however many you kill, you will fail.

DEATH UNDERNEATH THE ARCHES

Before they were converted into luxurious apartments, the dock buildings, warehouses and factories around the Thames were too strategic a target for the Luftwaffe to ignore. Bermondsey suffered some of the heaviest bombing of the Blitz, being hit repeatedly more times than any other place in the UK, and the casualties were high. Much of this is, of course, documented in the Blitz Experience at Churchill House on Tooley Street, but a short walk away two archways are a more sombre reminder of the war.

Druid Street Arch and Stainer Street Arch were both used as makeshift bomb shelters during the war and sadly both were hit by German bombs.

Druid's Arch housed a social club and billiards hall by day, but each evening it was converted into a shelter. One night in October 1940 it suffered a direct hit and 87 people were killed, making it the single worst disaster in Southwark's history.

Less than six months later another hit in the area resulted in a lower death toll, but a more grisly legacy. In February 1941, 68 people lost their lives in an explosion at Stainer's Arch. Many of their bodies were never recovered from the rubble and they lay entombed there to this day.

DOWN AND OUT ON TOOLEY STREET

It's difficult to say what George Orwell would make of twenty-first-century London, with its CCTV and its inhabitants' love of a telescreen programme called *Big Brother*, but it's a safe bet to say that he wouldn't recognise his old stomping ground. Back in the days when he was still known as Eric Arthur Blair he lived for some time on Tooley Street while writing *Down and Out in Paris and London* (1933). His experiences here not only made it into that book, but also provided fodder for *A Clergyman's Daughter* (1935).

These days, of course, Tooley Street is full of tourists making their way from London Bridge Station, the London Dungeon and Tower Bridge. The doss houses or 'kips' he wrote about and stayed in are long gone and replaced with trendy businesses and upmarket apartments.

Interestingly enough, it was Tooley Street that saw the first ominous black poles appear in the area. These unexpected structures were soon blossoming with cameras and a range of monitoring devices, not just on Tooley Street but in 21 other spots too, to build a state-of-the-art surveillance zone. This turned out to be part of a new Congestion Zone trial to try to find a more efficient way of keeping tabs on the city's cars. If the technology wasn't enough to make Orwell wince then the £2.5 million price tag certainly would have. If the trial is deemed a success then the poles may spread outwards to keep an eye on more Winston Smiths.

10 FACTS ABOUT THE SOUTH BANK THAT MAY NOT BE TRUE

1 *An American Werewolf in London* is based on the true story of an American tourist who was killed while running naked down Clink Street by the SAS in 1979.

2 'The South Bank Show' was actually broadcast from an old punk venue in Wigan, Lancashire, called The Den.

3 Relocating the Thames to the southern hemisphere would immediately force the South Bank to become the North Bank due to the Coriolis effect.

4 Before the design of the London Eye was settled as a wheel, blueprints were drawn up for a revolving triangle that would have been known as the Venus.

5 The National Theatre can transform into a giant robot if attacked. The robot's name is Brutus Londoninius and it carries a 50ft Roman sword.

6 In order to convert the power station that is now the Tate Modern, 17 art galleries throughout the UK had to be converted into power stations.

7 Shakespeare shares the unhappy distinction of having only one globe with frustrated artist Adolph Hitler.

8 The Oxo Tower is all that remains of an axis of food storage buildings destroyed during World War II, the others being the Bovril and Bisto Towers.

9 Up until 1976 several Thames Television stars such as Sid James faced compulsorily baptisms in the river beneath Tower Bridge.

10 Raw sewage pumped into the Thames actually smells sweeter as it passes by the South Bank but regains its natural odour once it reaches the Millennium Dome.

The filthiest, the strangest, the most extraordinary of the many localities that are hidden in London...
Charles Dickens on Shad Thames in *Oliver Twist* (1837-38)

PALE CHILDREN ESPECIALLY WELCOME

The largest green space on the South Bank is the nine acres given over to Archbishop's Park close to Waterloo Station. The space is made up of gardens once belonging to Lambeth Palace, but that all changed in 1901 when good old Archbishop Tait donated the land to the 'scores of pale children' who lived nearby. The park also contained an-air raid shelter during World War II that gave families a refuge from German doodlebugs and V2 rockets. These days it simply offers a quiet place to get away from the hustle and bustle of Waterloo's 75 million commuters per year.

Plans for a face-lift are underway, with the wooden play area being transformed into a half-buried pirate ship and even the putting green being given over to more child-friendly space: a dry river bed linking the new play areas. Sporty types will continue to find a home here with resurfaced pitches, while those who prefer to get fat in the sun can head for the new picnic areas. Everyone can be confident that staff at nearby St Thomas' hospital will be on hand to help out with the occasional heart attack.

NOT YOUR AVERAGE GRAFFITI ARTIST

Polish-born artist Feliks Topolski was one of the first to establish a studio on the South Bank back in 1951, at the time of the Festival of Britain. He had spent some time during World War II as an official war artist and his work is in the collection of the nearby Tate gallery. The best place to sample the Topolski experience, however, is to be found not in a gallery but beneath a bridge.

Topolski set to work on his *Memoir of the 20th Century* in 1975 and was still working on it some 14 years later when he died. *Memoir* spans some 600ft in length and because of its unusual location beneath the arches of Hungerford Bridge varies in height from 12ft to 20ft. It chronicles some of the most important moments and historical figures from the twentieth century including Mahatma Gandhi, George Bernard Shaw, Picasso, Martin Luther King and Laurence Olivier.

This amazing one-of-a-kind mural, owned by the South Bank Centre, fell into disrepair mostly due to its damp location. But a recent award of a £1 million grant from the Heritage Lottery Fund will ensure its survival as an important part of London's artistic wealth.

Further down the Thames, work by notorious street artist Banksy has been whitewashed away, showing how fine the line remains between art and vandalism.

TOWER SUBWAY

Visitors and Londoners alike love Tower Bridge, but very few of them give a thought to what lies beneath. No, not just the Thames... In 1869, before the bridge was built, another Victorian engineering wonder was already in place: the Tower Subway. This tunnel, constructed almost exactly below where Tower Bridge now stands, was the world's first underground tube railway. For a short time an omnibus service (actually a cable car) took up to 12 passengers at a time under the river, before the tunnel was converted into a pedestrian walkway allowing Londoners to stroll by gaslight under the Thames. Once Tower Bridge opened the subway couldn't compete and it fell into disuse. Despite a brief episode of infamy when a man with a knife was spotted there at the height of Jack the Ripper's reign of terror the walkway was closed to the public in 1896.

If you take a moment to look around before joining the throngs at the Tower of London you can easily spot a small squat chimney-like structure at Tower Hill (on the north side of the bridge). This is the entrance kiosk to the subway built in 1926 by the London Hydraulic Water Company, who took over use of the tunnel to run their hydraulics. The tunnel survived bomb damage during the Blitz and is still used today to run fibre optics beneath the murky waters. So despite its towering successor it still plays an active, if slightly less romantic and unsung role, in many Londoners' lives.

LONDON SOUTH BANK UNIVERSITY
HONORARY DEGREE HOLDERS

Mr Kevin Spacey Doctor of Letters

Mr Benjamin Zephaniah Doctor of Letters

Ms Esther Rantzen Doctor of Literature

Lord Melvyn Bragg of Wigton Doctor of Literature

Dame Diana Rigg Doctor of Literature

Miss Zoe Wanamaker Doctor of Literature

Reverend Desmond Tutu Doctor of Law

Sir Michael Caine Doctor of Literature

Mr Richard Briers OBE Doctor of Literature

Sir Trevor McDonald OBE Doctor of Literature

THINGS YOU CAN'T SEE NO MATTER HOW HARD YOU TRY

The River Neckinger – It's subterranean.

Crossbones graveyard – There are no markers for it.

U155 – Although this World War I German U-boat sailed through Tower Bridge and was displayed in London, it was broken up in 1922.

Where Sir Christopher Wren stayed during the building of St Paul's cathedral – The plaque on Cardinal's Wharf between the Tate Modern and the Globe Theatre is a fib.

Jacobs Island – The notorious setting of *Oliver Twist* is now lost in the picturesque Shad Thames.

The Bear Gardens Museum – It was replaced with the Globe Education Centre, which does have a large stuffed bear in its foyer.

A cinema on Tower Bridge Road – Although in the past there were four: The Electric, the Super, the Tower and the Trocette.

The crystal-blue Thames – As seen in the *Thunderbirds* movie. It was cleaned up with CGI.

The flooded moat around the Tower of London – Although plans are afoot to refill it for the first time since 1830.

LONDON BRIDGE VS. THE VIKINGS

The Victorian Gothic façade of Tower Bridge may leave the less ornate London Bridge in the shade, but it's the simpler crossing that leaves Tower Bridge standing in the history stakes. Rebuilt numerous times, London Bridge has been present in one form or another for 2,000 years. Perhaps most famously, in the late 1960s it was shipped to America and rebuilt in Arizona by Robert P McCulloch.

Not everyone has been as reverent to the crossing though. In 1013 Southwark was a Danish stronghold known as Sudvirke. King Ethelred, desperate for help against the Danes, turned to Olaf Haraldsson who was more than happy to sail up the Thames with his Vikings. They manoeuvred their longboats under London Bridge and fastened ropes around the supports. By rowing downstream as hard as they could they eventually pulled the bridge and most of the Danish garrison with them. This tale of derring-do was recounted in the Heimskringla saga which also contained a song featuring the lines: 'London Bridge is broken down [...]/ Gold is won, and bright renown [...]/ Odin makes our Olaf win!'

The Fair Lady of the more modern nursery rhyme only came into popular use after 1269 when Queen Eleanor spent the money for repairing the bridge on something more frivolous.

FILMS SHOT IN THE SOUTH BANK AREA INCLUDE:

Mission Impossible – MI5 apparently have a helicopter pad just in front of Tower Bridge.

The Man Who Haunted Himself – Doomed City big shot Roger Moore in his favourite role crosses London Bridge.

The Man Who Knew Too Much – The original Hitchcock from 1934 has an early establishing shot of London using, you guessed it, Tower Bridge.

Lock Stock and Two Smoking Barrels – Mockney gangsters have now made way for Paul Smith at 13 Park Street on the edge of Borough Market

Thunderbirds – Despite CGI elsewhere, that was a real helicopter flying under Tower Bridge.

An American Werewolf in London – the SAS blow poor David Kessler away on Clink Street.

Bridget Jones's Diary – Borough Market constantly proves itself a popular movie haunt. See also *The French Lieutenant's Woman*, *Howards End* and *Entrapment*.

Tomb Raider – Angelina Jolie takes her backside zooming across Tower Bridge on a motorcycle.

Love Actually – Hugh Grant and co. clock up almost as many locations as DVD rentals, including the Millennium Bridge, Gabriels Wharf, the Oxo Tower, the Tate Modern, City Hall and the London Eye.

Split Second – How to establish that Rutger Haur is going to clean up London? Have him zoom across Tower Bridge of course.

Harry Potter and the Prisoner of Azkaban – The Leaky Cauldron is on Stoney Street near Borough Market.

The Constant Gardener – Ralph Fiennes and Rachel Weisz meet at a lecture in the Tate Modern.

The Mummy Returns – Filming on Tower Bridge caused such disruption that the police had to step in.

ROLL OUT THE BARRELS

Despite being the definition of gentrification, Shad Thames is still as much a maze of distraction as it was when Dickens wrote about it. You're less likely to be snatched by Oliver Reed and dangled from a warehouse walkway, but you should still keep your eyes open.

Wandering around the now very spruce converted warehouses is a jaw-dropper – not just because of the property prices in the local estate agents' windows, but also because of all the original features that still adorn the buildings. Most warehouses stored spices so many still bear the names of their prior stores, making them a sweeter-smelling proposition than the former tannery buildings scattered on the other side of Tower Bridge.

Look up and you'll see the original walkways crisscrossing from building to building – these were originally used to roll barrels between the warehouses. These runs have now been incorporated into the private flats that make up so much of the buildings. Most are used as balconies and provide a unique way for neighbours of otherwise unconnected buildings to meet and despair at the tourist types swarming below at the weekends. Give them a wave.

CROSSBONES

There's an empty plot of land just off Redcross Way in SE1 that sports a unique memorial. A makeshift wall of London Underground boards designed to keep people out has been appropriated for messages and the occasional scrawled skull and crossbones, while further along a weathered gate is covered in colourful ribbons. Welcome to Crossbones.

Crossbones has never been recognised as an official graveyard, despite the staggering number of bodies buried here from medieval times up until 1853. In the 1990s archaeologists from the Museum of London partially excavated the site just before an electricity substation for the Jubilee Line Extension was built. Almost 150 skeletons were removed – only an estimated 1% of the graveyard's occupants.

So who were these poor unfortunates? For the most part they were 'single women': a quaint euphemism for the prostitutes who filled the brothels of Bankside. Their work was more often than not legal, but the Church refused them a burial. Those that repented were forgiven, leaving the unrepentant to Crossbones.

Transport for London plans to develop the site, but a grassroots campaign exists to ensure that the graveyard is not forgotten. A small group of local people meet here on the 23rd of each month to tidy the area and remember what they call 'The Outcast Dead'.

•

HYDE PARK
AND CHELSEA

•

HYDE PARK AND CHELSEA

A DRAINING EXPERIENCE

The Princess Diana Memorial Fountain in Hyde Park has had something of a chequered history, to say the least. It's basically a circular trench that has a fast-flowing stream passing around it, and it opened to a mixed reaction. Architecture critics called it bland and uninspired; arch-traditionalists disliked its modernity and abstraction. Both these sides derided it as a ditch or a drain.

It had significantly more success with the general public, who loved it. Its great appeal was interactivity, in that people could sit around it on a warm day and paddle, and children loved to play in it.

This popularity proved to be much more damaging than the sniffy critical reaction. After three people slipped and hurt themselves, the fountain was closed for a while. It also broke and flooded, once after its pumps failed, and again when it became clogged with falling leaves – a park-based hazard that the designers apparently neglected to appreciate.

The fountain/stream/drain has now been altered to stop it posing a threat to the kiddies, to help defend it against the leaf menace, and to protect the surrounding lawns from becoming a mudbath. It is quite a pleasant sight on a summer's day, but you might want to bring wellies and a hard hat.

... AND WHILE WE'RE ON THE SUBJECT OF DIANA ...

No one has been quite so relentlessly memorialised as Diana, Princess of Wales. As well as the Memorial Fountain, a variety of other places have been dedicated to her in perpetuity: there's a memorial walk in Hyde Park; the 'DianaLand' theme park set up by her brother in Althorp; the impromptu shrine at the Pont de l'Alma in Paris, where she met her end; and the front page of the *Daily Express*. On top of that are the commemorative tubs of margarine and scratchcards endorsed by the trust that safeguards the Princess's name from tacky commercialisation.

But one particularly touching tribute to the late Princess can be found in Harrods in Knightsbridge. The store's proprietor, Mohammed al Fayed, lost his son Dodi in the accident that killed Diana, and has set up his own devotional site to the couple within the hallowed halls of the corner shop. It's quite a sight. But it's not a scratch on what Chairman Mo has planned for himself.

Al Fayed is believed to be planning a mausoleum for himself on the roof of the world-famous department store – as is his right, as owner, planning laws permitting. Extraordinary as it may sound, this is not the first time such a scheme has been proposed. Henry Gordon Selfridge wanted a truly colossal monumental mausoleum tower to be built above the Oxford Street store that bears his name. Plans were drawn up for this monstrous 25-storey edifice in 1918, but never came to pass. Let's hope Mo has more luck.

SPEAKERS' CORNER: WHERE REALITY MEETS THE FICTIONAL

Famous people from fact and fiction who honed their arguments in the north-east corner of Hyde Park.

Karl Heinrich Marx, political philosopher and economist
Al Bundy, shoe salesman and father in *Married with Children*
Vladimir Ilyich Lenin, communist revolutionary and premier
King Mob, anarchist, assassin and pop star in *The Invisibles*
Eric Arthur Blair aka **George Orwell**, author and journalist
A priest, spots Damien as the Beast in *The Omen*
William Morris, author, designer and craftsman
Cory Doctorow, famous blogger and copyleftist

ATLANTIS
AND THE CIRCLE LINE

The Greek Philosopher Plato described the lost city of Atlantis as being girdled by a mighty series of harbours linked by a system of bridges and tunnels. Any Londoner, upon reading this, will immediately realise that he was actually referring to the Circle line. And because we know where London is, Atlantis isn't Lost. It's probably just trying to find its way to the Waterloo & City line from the Circle line platforms at Monument.

Consider the facts. The Circle line has long held a mystical power over London. Its doings are the stuff of legend, and its services are often mythical (a signal failure on the Circle can bring chaos to three other lines, and I'd like to see the Waterloo & City try that).

Of course, it isn't really a circle – its circuit is more of a squashed oval, but the name Oval was already taken by a station on the Northern line and Circle had much more of a ring to it.

The area's canals and harbours were drained long ago to make way for a much more up-to-date system of railways, but if you consider the presence of waterways at Sloane Square (the Westbourne) and Farringdon (the Fleet), and the frequency with which some stations flood, it's only a matter of time before the ancient watercourse reclaims its former route, now only remembered in station names such as Bays*water,* Embankment, Great *Port*land Street and Liver*pool* Street.

With this information in mind, a journey on the Circle is utterly transformed. Kensington High Street has more than a hint of classical ruin to it, and Gloucester Road is right out of the Temple of Doom. If they ever display Golden Tribal Fetishes of Unknown Origin on the Platform for Art, expect blow darts and rolling boulders to be part of the security features.

COURT SHORT
There's a secret entrance into the Royal Court Theatre on Sloane Square. If you go into the centre of the square there is a flight of steps leading down into what was once a gentlemen's public lavatory. Now, those steps lead down into the Royal Court restaurant, which was excavated out under the street during the theatre's massive turn-of-the-millennium modernisation. It was meant to be an alternative entrance to the restaurant, a plan needlessly stymied by the local council.

Another lavatorial Royal Court fact: before the modernisation, from the front two rows of the auditorium you could hear the toilets flushing in the dressing rooms.

THE PLAYING FIELDS OF SW3

Ask any non-Chelsea supporter and they'll attest that the blue-clad corinthians of Stamford Bridge have something of a superiority complex. This may be because deep down they consider themselves to be the only London team — for a while the club was going to be called London FC, despite being a relative newcomer to the capital. But there is a special part of London in the club's history: the Stamford Bridge ground was built on rubble excavated from the Metropolitan Line.

A FLICK THROUGH THE HARRODS CATALOGUE

Barbecue (£2,795). Watch your money go up in smoke with the Napoleon PT600. Includes 'ergonomic designer knobs'.

Croquet set (£489). Curiously filed under 'Men's essentials', the Jaques Edenbrige Croquet Set will keep up to six people entertained. As would the 32 pints of ale the same money could buy for each person.

Posh kids' clobber. At £129, the boys' check blazer can be fitted to precocious children aged 4-16.

Novelty cheese knife (£49.54). A mouse-handled bit of cutlery that 'offers a child-like quality with an inherent depth of meaning'. It also cuts cheese. Very expensively.

Hot water-bottle cover (£49). For the fortunately niche market of people who just can't absorb enough heat from all the sodding piles of money they have to burn.

Coffee machine (£3,500). Has 20 different settings. No, you can't have tea.

Ironing board (£599). In case the maid's sick.

Iron (£399). Why not spend the full grand and get a top-of-the-range steam iron to complement your board? Comes with the tag line 'Make the most of life'. Ironing's the new rock 'n' roll, you know.

Flaky Itchy shampoo (£38). That's really what it's called. Cheers, guys, don't pull your punches. Leaves your hair shiny and your wallet bare.

Afternoon tea bags (£5.95). Let's face it, this is what you've come for, isn't it?

400 – Number of complaints about swearing received by the BBC after the Live 8 concert in 2005.

351 – number of acres the park covers.

107 – width in feet of the park's grand entrance.

2.2 million – number of pounds that the Princess Diana Memorial Fountain went over budget.

27 – number of incidents of 'male importuning' reported in the park in 1962.

150,000 – the official attendance figures for the record-breaking Queen gig in 1976. The real number is thought to be closer to 180,000.

1 – The number of people who've died during the annual Christmas Morning swim in the Serpentine.

300 – the number of oil lamps it took to to make Rotten Row the first artificially lit highway in Britain when it opened in 1690.

A PENCHANT FOR PENSIONERS

One very distinctive sight of this area is the smart red coats of the Chelsea Pensioners, elderly ex-servicemen who are given lodgings by the Royal Hospital in Chelsea.

The hospital was set up in the later years of the seventeenth century to care for veterans of the Civil War. The Civil War had made extensive use of standing armies and professional soldiers, and thus professional soldiers at the end of their careers didn't have their 'old' livelihoods or farms to return to. Some form of welfare was required.

Money was something of a problem in the early years of the operation, and innovative solutions had to be found. Christopher Wren (yes, that Wren), who designed the hospital buildings, suggested that the licence fees paid by hackney carriages could fund it, but that never worked. The city of Newcastle sent 100 wagons of coal a year under a deal struck with Charles II – they didn't have to pay rent on their castle in return.

The grounds of the Royal Hospital have one striking indicator of its military heritage: two batteries of guns, including four captured from the French at Waterloo and others snatched from the Dutch, the Sikhs and the Chinese.

Britain's first televised church service was broadcast from the chapel in 1949.

TAKING A TURNER FOR THE WORST JMW Turner lived in Chelsea, near the river that he loved to paint. He was so keen on gazing at the Thames that he had a balcony added to his home so he could watch it quietly flowing by in the evenings.

He also died in Chelsea, but not in that particular house. Instead, the painter of *The Fighting Téméraire* died at the house of his mistress in 1851. His cause of death was recorded as 'natural decay' – understandable, as he was 76. A few years later, several of his drawings were destroyed by the National Gallery on the grounds that they were extremely obscene.

> **They turned back towards Oakley Street. The lamps and the plane-trees, following the line of the embankment, struck a note of dignity that is rare in English cities... There is something Continental about Chelsea Embankment.**
>
> EM Forster, *Howards End* (1910)

SPLASH!

A variety of things have ended up in the Serpentine, the lake at the centre of Hyde Park. Most notably, there is the Serpentine Swimming Club, established in 1864, which conducts a race every Christmas Day. The water temperature on the day is typically only four degrees above freezing, but so far there has only been one death. The more timid can still enjoy pleasure boats in summer.

In 1814, the Serpentine was used to stage an impressive mock naval battle to commemorate the Battle of the Nile between the British Navy and Napoleon's forces. For some reason, however, the 'French' ships carried American colours.

Less entertainingly, Harriet Westbrook, the first wife of Percy Bysshe Shelley, drowned herself in the lake in 1816.

The lake also serves as a potential punishment for those who displease the crowds at Speakers' Corner, as George Bernard Shaw noted in his play *The Simpleton of the Unexpected Isles*: 'A Hyde Park orator was thrown into the Serpentine for saying that the British Empire was not the only pebble on the beach. He has been fined thirty shillings for being in unlawful possession of a life buoy, the property of the Royal Humane Society.'

Aristocratic Fascist sympathiser Unity Mitford almost suffered this fate in 1938 when she was spotted at a Labour party rally, but managed to evade her pursuers.

TYBURN

The Tyburn, one of the lost rivers of London, still flows from Swiss Cottage beneath Bayswater, Hyde Park, Westminster and Pimlico.

Its name, however, carries a far more sinister meaning for London. Tyburn, a spot near what is now Marble Arch, was the site of London's most notorious gallows, and was synonymous with the executioner's grim art. Public executions were a popular diversion in seventeenth- and eighteenth-century London, and tended to attract large and boisterous crowds.

As the deadly spot was in the parish of Paddington, days when there would be particularly enjoyable executions were known as Paddington Fair Days, and the final jerks and spasms of the condemned were referred to as 'dancing the Paddington frisk'. Among those who danced the Paddington frisk at Tyburn was the notorious highwayman Dick Turpin. Although it is now one of London's most upscale residential areas, the road west from the city was at the time infested by robbers.

In a similar vein, young thieves or pickpockets were called 'Tyburn Blossoms', as they would 'in time ripen into fruit borne by the deadly never-green' (*The 1811 Dictionary of the Vulgar Tongue*) – in other words, swing from the gallows, which could accommodate up to eight people at a time.

Hanging was not the only form of death seen at Tyburn – women were burned at the stake there as late as the 1720s. The last woman to meet this end was Catherine Hayes, a pub landlady. She cut up her husband and threw his head into the Thames in 1726, and distributed his other parts around the city. Appropriately, the name of her pub was the Gentleman in Trouble.

Nothing remains of the execution site now, other than an easy-to-miss marker in the middle of the road.

Further to the west, along Bayswater Road, is the Tyburn Convent. It's a distinctive red-brick building with a curved façade and a very fine carving of Christ on the Cross overhanging the street. If you look carefully, you will see an incredibly narrow building wedged between the convent and its left-hand neighbour, built from the same red brick. This is London's smallest house, only a shade wider than its own front door. The ground floor is entirely taken up by a staircase leading to the first floor, and the first floor can only accommodate a narrow single bed. Despite London's shortage of affordable housing, this des res is at present unoccupied.

Sir Humphrey Appleby: **Very well, if you walked into a nuclear missile showroom you would buy Trident – it's lovely, it's elegant, it's beautiful. It is quite simply the best. And Britain should have the best. In the world of the nuclear missile it is the Savile Row suit, the Rolls Royce Corniche, the Château Lafitte 1945. It is the nuclear missile Harrods would sell you. What more can I say?**

Jim Hacker: **Only that it costs £15 billion and we don't need it.**

Sir Humphrey Appleby: **Well, you can say that about anything at Harrods.**

From an episode of *Yes, Prime Minister* (series 1), first aired in 1986

THE PARK THAT WON'T STAY PARKED

Hyde Park's a tricksy place. Its features never seem to sit still for long. Take the two eastern corners. To the north there's Nash's Marble Arch, which started life as a ceremonial gateway to Buckingham Palace before being exiled to the sorry traffic island it decorates today. It may yet move again, to Speakers' Corner. Then there's the Wellington Arch in the south-east corner. In 1883, this made comparatively timid progress by shifting just a few feet to the right. Its crowning statue of the Iron Duke was more adventurous, fleeing to Aldershot.

Then, of course, there's the Crystal Palace, built to the south of Hyde Park for the Great Exhibition of 1851. Afterwards, the huge greenhouse was transported over to Sydenham, where it burned down some decades later.

And on it goes. Cumberland Lodge moved west, then west again. The statue of St George also headed west, presumably in search of dragons. And the stone fountain of a boy and dolphin shifted from Park Lane to Regent's Park before finally settling down near Hyde Park Corner.

If we're counting Kensington Gardens, the litany of itinerants continues. We finish with Queen Anne's alcove, designed by Wren. This peripatetic porch made the trek in 1868 from the south of the park to its current location near Bayswater Road, after becoming a hangout for unsavoury types.

Now, about that Diana fountain...

I'LL HAVE WHAT HE'S HAVING

There are plenty of stories to be told about the King's Road of the 1960s, with its decadent cavalcade of rock stars, fashion designers, footballers and screen icons.

One of the best is almost undoubtedly apocryphal but bears repeating, if only because there haven't been many Mick Jagger stories worth retelling for quite a while now.

The story goes that the Rolling Stones frontman was dining in one of the more chic eateries on the King's Road when a fellow diner, somewhat confused and appalled by the singer's long hair and pouty lips, felt compelled to enquire of Mick whether he was of the male or female sex.

Mick (or Sir Mick as he is today) decided to end the confusion by standing up in the middle of the restaurant, unzipping his flies and bearing his manhood to one and all.

RIVERS AND CAVE-INS UNDER SLOANE SQUARE

If you look up while waiting for a train at Sloane Square station, you might be able to see a large iron pipe. That pipe contains the Westbourne river, one of London's 'lost' watercourses, on its much-diminished passage to the Thames. The pipe is directly connected to the Serpentine in Hyde Park, which is also part of the stream's course.

Sloane Square station was also the site of one of the worst bomb hits of the Blitz. It was being used as a shelter in 1940 when the eastbound district line tunnel received a direct hit, collapsing the tunnel roof on top of a train as it left the platform.

HYDE AND GO SEEK

Hyde Park, Adelaide – an Australian suburb
Hyde Park, Colombo – focal point for Sri Lanka's labour movement
Hyde Park, Gauteng – a South African suburb
Hyde Park, London – The original, and dare we say best?
Hyde Park, Leeds – innercity space beloved of student types
Hyde Park, Perth – a Western Australian park
Hyde Park, Sydney – a New South Wales park
Hyde Parks, USA – more than 30 of them spread across America

THE 'B' IN 'KGB' IS FOR BROMPTON

Brompton Oratory is one of the most beautiful and oft-ignored churches in London. It's a Catholic foundation, built in the late nineteenth century in perfect Italianate style with a magnificent interior: a scrap of Venice or Florence in the museum district.

One group that did not overlook it, however, was the KGB. They found that a niche between two columns, tucked behind a statue, made an ideal 'dead letter drop' – a place where secret messages or microfilms could be dropped by covert agents and later picked up by Soviet embassy staff for transmission back to Moscow. Secret Intelligence Service officer Kim Philby lived nearby, and may have been among those who used it.

NOTTING HILL
AND THE WEST

NOTTING HILL AND THE WEST

THE BLOODY BATTLES OF BRENTFORD

West London has seen a fair amount of warfare, and for some reason, Brentford has a particularly bloody history. It is thought to be the place where the invading Roman armies crossed the River Thames in their conquest of Britain, meeting the armies of the British chieftain Cassibellaun on the north bank. A key source for this story is the chronicler Geoffrey of Monmouth, who is wholly unreliable and invented many stories to lend weight to his claim that London was founded by the Trojan Brutus as 'New Troy', or 'Trinovantum'.

A better-documented engagement took place in 1016 between another invader, this time King Cnut of Denmark, and the defending forces of Edmund Ironside.

This bloody field – it is now partly in the grounds of Syon House, but otherwise has been built over – was again the scene of armed struggle in 1642, during the Civil War. Parliamentarians, who were defending London against the advancing Royalists, fought a small battle there as a delaying action, while the bulk of their armies gathered to the east. Meanwhile, the King's men sacked Brentford, which must have been great fun, but did great harm to their cause, with tales of the violence spreading throughout the city. The Roundheads and London's own defence force were able to halt the advancing army at Turnham Green the following day.

A few months ago I spent the night bonking the Welsh Ladies
Kickboxing Champion in a caravan somewhere beyond
Hammersmith. She said that the whole of London seemed like one
vast rat's maze to her. I'd said yes, but what if the rats happened
to like being in the maze?

David Mitchell, *Ghostwritten* (1999)

DYSFUNCTIONAL STATIONS

West London's tube stations just can't seem to get it together. If you want to get from Edgware Road station (District, Circle and Hammersmith & City lines) to Edgware Road station (Bakerloo line), you have to leave the place, go down Chapel Street, turn right onto Edgware Road, walk under the Westway and then re-enter another station. Similarly, at Hammersmith, to change from the District or Piccadilly lines to the Hammersmith & City line, you have to leave one station, walk through a shopping centre, cross a busy road junction, walk down the street a bit and then re-enter another one. It's an equally tedious rigmarole at Paddington station if you want to go between the Hammersmith & City and Bakerloo lines. Also, if you want to go between Shepherd's Bush (Hammersmith & City line) and Shepherd's Bush (Central line), it's about 383 yards up the Uxbridge Road between the two stations. Talk about beating around the Bush.

Harry Beck's notoriously misleading (but beautiful) tube map has attempted to deal with this dysfunction in a variety of ways. Some versions depict most of the stations as a linked interchange – an outright lie – while others, such as Hammersmith (Hammersmith & City), are shown as an interchange blob, but not interchanging with anywhere. At least Shepherd's Bush is honest, it is always shown as two separate stations. Even some stations that now serve as true interchanges were initially two separate stations. Notting Hill Gate, for example, was rebuilt in the 1940s to link the Central and District lines.

Why all this disharmony? The answer is simple. The various lines were all built by different companies, and getting them to cooperate was like herding cats. It's a miracle the Circle line was built at all. It was a rare joint venture by the Metropolitan and District firms, which explains its odd non-circular shape. It was not called the Circle line originally, but the Inner Circuit, which is appropriate as Beck's topological tube map is based on an electrical circuit.

133

SUMP'N'STEAMY? SOUNDS FISHY

A great place to visit in west London is the Kew Bridge Steam Museum, on Green Dragon Lane, by Kew Bridge station (mainline; the closest tube is the District line at Gunnersbury).

The mighty steam-powered pumps in this attractive Victorian building supplied central London with fresh water. Now, it is a splendid temple to steam, housing the world's largest collection of steam pumps and London's only operational steam railway. Many of the pumps are still functioning, and are fired up at the weekend. The railway, a narrow gauge affair, runs on Sundays from March until November every year. It is one of the capital's most underrated attractions, and was refurbished in 2005 for its 30th birthday.

One interesting and unique sight in the museum is its piscine inhabitants – some goldfish who live in the sump of one of the engines (a Boulton & Watt, since you ask). The goldfish were introduced to replace a well-known and much-loved river fish that had somehow found its way in there. This icthyoid intruder was believed to have been either a carp or perch, and was so missed upon its demise that the replacements were introduced.

HoHo!

William Hogarth, the artist and moral chronicler of London in the eighteenth century, lived in Chiswick until his death in 1764. He was best known for his series of prints *Rake's Progress*, which chronicle the downfall of a degenerate Georgian Londoner, and the engraving *Gin Lane*, which depicts the ruin caused by drink.

Hogarth was something of a difficult character. He hated foreigners in general, especially the French, and wasn't overly keen on his fellow countrymen, either. He was once commissioned to paint the portrait of a particularly unattractive aristocrat, and he did so with unabashed realism. According to Mark Bryant's book *Private Lives*, 'the finished picture so offended the sitter that he refused to pay for it – whereupon Hogarth threatened to embellish it with a tail and other appendages and sell it for display in a freak show: the nobleman promptly paid up, took the picture away and burnt it'.

You can still see Hogarth's House in Chiswick. In fact, the building is quite hard to miss, because it's on Hogarth Lane, just off the Hogarth roundabout. The house, now a museum, is referred to as HoHo by some Chiswick natives.

BLUE BRIGADES BATTER BADDERS

Hounslow appears in the *Quatermass* science fiction series, but don't expect the local council to set up a tourist trail any time soon. In *The Quatermass Conclusion*, the borough is described as 'one of the worst no-go areas' in a devastated, Balkanised future London, ripped apart by gang warfare between the 'Blue Brigade' and the 'Badders'. Our hero, Professor Bernard Quatermass, almost gets tangled up in this conflict as he rushes across London to warn people at Wembley Stadium about a nefarious alien plot. It's not all bad, though, as the gang rites of this dystopia appear to involve strong, bare-chested female role models.

Another fictional dystopia can be found in the fringes of west London. The campus of Uxbridge University can be seen in Stanley Kubrick's *A Clockwork Orange*. It's the research centre where Alex is brainwashed into becoming a 'model citizen'.

THE NEXT NOTTING HILLS

International locations revealed by a Google search for 'equivalent to Notting Hill'

Strathbungo, Glasgow

West Didsbury, Manchester

South Street, Philadelphia

Paddington, Sydney

The Marais, Paris

Ponsonby, Auckland

The 'Golden Triangle', Norwich

Christianshavn, Copenhagen

Campo Dei Fiore, Rome

PERIVALE SUCKS

One of the finest art deco buildings in the country can be seen in Perivale, and it is the Hoover Building. Indeed, it's hard to miss, because the former vacuum cleaner factory, workshop and offices are palatial in scale and completely dominate the A40 as it winds out of London. The building is clad in gleaming white concrete and decorated with Egyptian-style coloured tiles. It really is spectacular, far more impressive and beautiful than, say, Buckingham Palace. At night, it is lit up in green, and can even be seen by passengers in planes flying into Heathrow.

THE TARDIS AND THE ESCALATOR

The world's first escalator was installed at Earl's Court underground station in 1911, to serve the newly built Piccadilly line. It was feared that some people might be wary of using a moving staircase, so a one-legged man, called 'Bumper' Harris, was employed to ride up and down on it all day in order to demonstrate its safety. The route taken by the Piccadilly line between South Kensington and West Kensington stations, via Earl's Court, runs directly underneath the District line. This route was originally meant to be the Deep District, a lower-level electrified back-up for the District line that had been approved by planners in 1897, but was never built, save for this small stretch.

Situated outside the station on Earl's Court Road is another form of hi-tech transport – a blue box reminiscent of the TARDIS in *Doctor Who*. Of course, this box is incapable of time travel, and isn't really an original police box. Instead, it was erected 10 years ago as part of an effort to revive the network with a hi-tech edge, presumably involving sonic screwdrivers.

Apparently, Earl's Court, the area, has more Australians living in it per square inch than Australia. Or at least it certainly feels that way.

NEVER PLAY DICE IN FULHAM

Back in west London's wilder days, certain parts had reputations far removed from their present status. For instance, the grand curved stucco terraces of Holland Park are consciously modelled on the path of the racecourse it was built over. The patrons of this racecourse were largely drawn from the slums around the nearby potteries; they were noted for being unusually vile creatures. This former Notting Hill lives on only as street names, including Hippodrome Place and Pottery Lane.

Portobello Road, renowned for its market, has an even more exotic history, dating back to the capture of Puerto Bello in Central America by Admiral Edward Vernon (1684-1757) in 1739. A farm west of London named itself 'Porto Bello' in a fit of national sentiment; the lane leading to it became 'Porto Bello Lane' and, later, the street we know now. Fulham has a similarly unusual association in its name. In the eighteenth century, its inhabitants obtained a reputation for manufacturing loaded dice. Theses loaded dice became know as 'Fulhams'.

> Like Wembley Stadium, Windows has become a global icon, so it's fitting that we are burying a copy for posterity beneath the pitch... if each line of code was represented by a blade of grass, the core software contained on just one computer would stretch like a blanket from goal line to halfway line.
>
> An unnamed spokesperson from Microsoft, commenting on a curious inclusion in the new stadium's time capsule

WEMBLEY'S EYEFUL

Wembley is now associated with footballing triumphs and disasters against our Continental friends and neighbours, but it could have been the site of an engineering triumph against the French. London's answer to the Eiffel Tower came very close to rising in Wembley Park. Many fanciful designs were put forward for the tower, each with one important common factor: they were all taller than their Parisian forebear. Some of the proposals were simply wacky. One went as far as to suggest dropping people in parachutes down the middle. Another eschewed vulgar steps and proposed employing mules to carry patrons up a long spiral ramp. The winning design was more conventional and construction began, but only the base was ever completed – and that was demolished in 1907.

GETTING THE HUMP

The Central line's deepest point is between Notting Hill Gate and Holland Park stations. The depth of the Central line – which was started in the 1890s – allowed it to employ an energy-saving device: the Earth's gravity. The stations were built on 'humps' in the line, higher than the rest of the track – a one-sixtieth upwards gradient helps the trains slow as they enter the station, and a one-thirtieth slope down helps them pick up speed as they leave. This innovation is now standard in underground railway design the world over.

A MUSICAL INTERLUDE

Requests received by the evening pianist in the High Street Kensington branch of McDonald's restaurant, which has been remodelled as a piano bar and internet cafe:

'Danny Boy', traditional

'Like a Virgin', Madonna

'Goodbye', Spice Girls

'Carwash', the Christina Aguilera version

'Torna a Surriento' and other Italian standards (requested by a homesick tourist)

And the tune the management requested him not to play because it was 'putting people off their food':

The theme from *Mission: Impossible*

BROMPTON'S BALLOONS AND BALLS

A good bit of London trivia to flummox people with is to get them to try to name all 10 Royal Parks. Battersea Park is a frequent (and erroneous) inclusion; but the one that is most often left out is Brompton Cemetery, which is located just south of Earl's Court Exhibition Centre and is the only Crown Cemetery.

It is home to more than 35,000 monuments, including two rather unusual military ones. General Alexander Anderson of the Royal Marine Light Infantry (1807-1877) is buried here in a grave that is covered in cannon balls. Elsewhere, Sub-Lieutenant Reginald Warneford (1892-1915) is commemorated. Warneford received the Victoria Cross for being the first man to shoot down a German zeppelin during World War I. His memorial has a fanciful carved relief of the exploding airship on it, and was paid for by the readers of the *Daily Express*. He is one of 13 holders of the VC in the cemetery.

Down the Vale he strolls, into Uxbridge Road, that sluggish, half-dead miserable thoroughfare of pawnshops and second-hand clothing, of limp fried fish, tired-out prostitutes, ugly newsagents and chemists whose main trade appears to be condoms and cures for piles, past Wood Lane's tall-tiered BBC which overlooks all this wretchedness with a kind of high-minded myopia, and crosses the littered scrub of Shepherd's Bush Green where half the condoms bought that night have already been used and discarded, to reach eventually Holland Park Avenue, its huge houses reminding him of grand nineteenth-century balls, of every possible elegance, of mysterious embassies, of scandal and terror and discreet detections, of enormously powerful tycoons who are superficially benign but actually plan to rule the world, perhaps the only avenue of its magnitude in London where the houses actually display their back, seated on elevated embankments, obscured by tall trees, by walls and hedges: Perhaps, like the BBC, disliking to look northward where Notting Dale begins, her slums more violently independent and thoroughly wicked than any Acton can create, where policemen patrol in threes or sometimes refuse to venture and taxi-drivers never go, which has created a population to match anything from the East End or Brixton yet a race distinct from all others, though even this is endangered by city planners who since the War make Standardisation one of their holy words.

Michael Moorcock,
Mother London (1988)

ICH BIN EIN HAMMERSMITHER

Hammersmith is twinned with West Berlin (as it was at the time). It is hard to detect any physical connections between the borough in west London and what is now half of the reunified German capital — but there is one very curious clue. And it can be found on the Mall by the River Thames, just to the west of Hammersmith Bridge. There is a West German lamppost bearing a plaque informing you that it was presented to Hammersmith by Willi Brandt (then West Berlin's mayor) in 1963.

MASSES FOR THE MASSES

Hounslow is home to the world's most populous Anglican parish, a parish that covers more than 61 million people. However, it has only one chapel, and you'd be hard-pressed to find it.

It's the chaplaincy of Heathrow, the world's busiest international airport, which has a curious little chapel underneath Terminal 2. If you are waiting for a delayed flight, it's worth taking a little bit of time to track it down. The design is curiously international, not to mention inter-denominational, and it's unlike any other church building. In fact, it more resembles a set from BBC sci-fi series *Blake's 7*. OK, so maybe it isn't St Peter's in Rome, but how many branches of Tie Rack can St Peter's offer? Answer me that.

SPOT THE THEME IN THESE BUILDING NAMES FROM AN ESTATE ON ST ANN'S ROAD

Dora House · Florence House
Dorrit House · Dombey House
Marley House · Pickwick House
Nickleby House

GREAT WEST ROAD LOSES FIZZ

Until recently, one of the most prominent landmarks on the Great West Road out of London was the plant where Lucozade, the fizzy energy drink, was made. The building itself was unremarkable, but it stood out thanks to the neon Lucozade sign on its side. This sign was a rare surviving piece of kinetic neon art from the 1950s, with pulsing lights illustrating an unending golden shower of the sticky glucose stuff. Beneath was the slogan 'LUCOZADE REPLACES LOST ENERGY'.

This, however, was not the original slogan. Its predecessor was rather hastily removed in the early 1980s when it became unexpectedly inappropriate. The original had read 'LUCOZADE AIDS RECOVERY'.

Sadly, the factory is now gone – it was demolished in 2004 to make way for the regional headquarters of Audi UK – and the sign may be lost for ever, despite vague hints that it may be re-erected on another prominent site nearby.

HOW TO PASS THROUGH 10 TUBE STATIONS STARTING WITH THE LETTER H WITHOUT LEAVING YOUR TRAIN

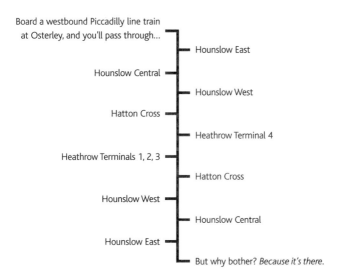

Board a westbound Piccadilly line train at Osterley, and you'll pass through...

Hounslow East

Hounslow Central

Hounslow West

Hatton Cross

Heathrow Terminal 4

Heathrow Terminals 1, 2, 3

Hatton Cross

Hounslow West

Hounslow Central

Hounslow East

But why bother? *Because it's there.*

STUFF TO WIND UP AMERICAN FANS OF THE FILM *NOTTING HILL* WITH

- Point out that Tobe Hooper's space vampire film *Lifeforce* is a much better flick.

- Say: 'Ohh, is that Julia Roberts?' in a loud voice just as they step off the kerb.

- Tell them the four seasons shot involved Hugh Grant moving very slowly for 12 months.

- Reveal to them that Ms Roberts's smile was all CGI and that it required 100 Cray supercomputers.

- Sell them any old blue door and claim it's the one from the movie.

- Sell them any passing fop who can't act and claim it's Hugh Grant.

HAMPSTEAD
AND THE NORTH

HAMPSTEAD
AND THE NORTH

WELCOME TO THE PLEASUREDOME

Brent Cross is where the rot started. If you've ever spent valuable hours of your life wondering what you were doing in a homogeneous enclosed air-conditioned temple to commerce, you can blame Brent Cross for importing the concept of the shopping mall over here.

It was the first major covered shopping centre to be built in the UK, opening in 1976, and although people were sceptical it would succeed, more than 50,000 people packed the centre every Saturday, visiting the 75 shops that comprised the original development. Nowadays, they reckon 19-20 million shoppers visit it each year. Regenerated in 1995, it currently contains 115 shops and cafés in which kids can scream 'I'm booooooooored!' while their parents completely ignore them.

Draft plans for further regeneration were approved in 2004, and interestingly, they turn the original concept inside out. The original premise was an indoor experience, but the proposals now speak of Brent Cross as 'an outward-looking development', with the enclosed malls becoming 'an integral part of the wider street network'. It seems the shopping centre is to become the town.

NORTH LONDON: SOME RANDOM, POINTLESS, NON-VITAL STATISTICS

- Most northerly tube station: Epping.

- Most northerly point within Greater London: Tilekiln Ossiers.

- Most northerly point within the M25: Winch Hill Wood.

- Most northerly borough: Enfield.

- Most bizarre place name: Botany Bay (Enfield), which is nowhere near any sizeable body of water.

- Worst disaster: Harrow train crash (1952); 112 killed.

- Greatest population born outside the UK: Brent (46.5%).

- Borough with the fewest tube stations: Hackney (zero).

- Lowest unemployment rate: Havering (3%).

- Borough with largest population: Barnet (327,000).

This place has a close relationship with the written word and has inspired hundreds of writers. I think that is why it was accepted – the Heath has a heritage intertwined with literature.

Giancarlo Neri, commenting in 2005 to *Camden New Journal* on his giant table and chair sculpture on Parliament Hill (now removed)

THE GREEN MAN OF CROUCH END

London's most elongated nature reserve can be found between Finsbury Park and Highgate, with a dogleg annexe running north-east to Alexandra Palace. This is the unimaginatively named Parkland Walk, which runs for four miles along the beds of a disused railway line.

As well as being a haven for wildlife, the Parkland Walk also offers rich pickings for fans of disused rail infrastructure. The dilapidated platforms of Crouch End station remain, along with a set of closed-off tunnels leading towards Highgate tube station.

Presiding over this rail graveyard, just east of the Crouch End station, is a larger-than-life troll-like figure (though, thinking about it, who actually knows what 'life-sized' is for a troll?), known in folklore as a 'green man'. His lithe body, with piercing eyes, is sculpted into an arched wall, as though he's somehow emerging from the brickwork. It's easy to imagine him sneaking about after dark, tending to his green kingdom, reclaimed from the railways.

FROZEN CHICKEN AND BACON

The endless chicken outlets of Holloway Road form something of a ley line of poultry. For if you follow the hill up to Highgate, you arrive at the site of what might be the world's first ever frozen chicken.

No, seriously.

And who was behind this breakthrough in avian storage? Bernard Matthews? Nope. Surely not Colonel Sanders? Certainly not. It was none other than Francis Bacon, the seventeenth-century philosopher and proto-scientist.

While climbing Highgate Hill one snowy day in 1626, Bacon was hit with the notion that meat might be protected from putrification through cold storage. No time like the present, thought Bacon, purchasing a fowl and stuffing it with the freshly fallen snow.

Sadly, while the chicken might have lasted for months, so preserved, Bacon did not. With all the feebleness of a Dickensian damsel exposed to some rain, the great man caught a chill and promptly dropped dead. It took another few hundred years before a certain Mr Birdseye finally got things right.

UPS AND DOWNS AT ALLY PALLY

Few buildings in the world can have a history of such fickle fortune as Alexandra Palace. Cursed and blessed in equal measure, the faded pile of Muswell Hill is the tragicomic, bricks-and-mortar equivalent of, say, Michael Barrymore.

Financial woes put a 15-year hiatus on construction; a delay of 'futuristic' quality for the normally industrious Victorians. But finally, in 1873, the north had a 'people's palace' to rival the doomed crystal cousin at Sydenham. It lasted two weeks. Fire gutted the complex and claimed three lives.

Somehow, it was rebuilt and reopened within two years. After several decades farting about with exhibitions and concerts, it was bought by the BBC. The Corporation stuck a monster antenna on top and began the first national television broadcasts. The facilities also came in handy a few years later for jamming German radio communications. Ally Pally was finally a success.

But not for long. The palace was again devastated by fire in 1980. Patched up, but never properly repaired, it's remained a semi-catatonic giant ever since, despite occasional attempts at resuscitation. Finally, another swing of fortune appears to be on the horizon as a major regeneration of the site seems likely. But with Ally Pally, you just never know what might happen.

TOP TRUMPS

GOLDERS GREEN CREMATORIUM **VS.** HIGHGATE CEMETERY

GOLDERS GREEN

Marc Bolan, *singer*
Songs about revolution: 1

Neville Chamberlain, *politician*
Signatures obtained on his piece of paper:
2 (his and Hitler's)

HG Wells, *writer*
Film adaptations of books starring
Tom Cruise: 1

Ronnie Scott, *jazz musician*
London institutions set up: 1

Rudyard Kipling, *writer*
Percentage of English-lit students
tortured through writings: 18%

Bernie Winters, *'entertainer'*
Dogs named Schnorbitz: 1

HIGHGATE

Karl Marx, *political philosopher*
Writings about revolution: lots

William Lovett, *Chartist*
Signatures obtained on second Chartist
petition: 3.25 million

Douglas Adams, *writer*
Film adaptations of books starring
Tom Cruise: 0 (low score wins)

William Alfred Foyle, *bookseller*
London institutions set up: 1

Charles Dickens, *writer*
Percentage of English-lit students
tortured through writings: 76%

Michael Faraday, *Scientist*
Dogs named Schnorbitz: 0

KILBURN ODDNESS

Kilburn is full of strange things. Perhaps the queerest of all, though, are two neighbours along Cambridge Avenue. First is a large, corrugated iron church like something out of the Wild West. Presumably it's a post-war prefab that never quite got replaced. The rusting, rustic hulk is now used as a scout hut, but looks like it might collapse at the merest sneeze.

Practically next door is a striking blue and white building associated with the RSPCA. Its strangeness is all in the signage above the door, which reads 'The Animal War Memorial Dispensary'. Fair enough, many animals have been killed in wars over the years and deserve the odd commemoration. But a 'dispensary' for memorials. Isn't that a trifle overkill?

SO MANY HAMPSTEADS, SO LITTLE TIME

Hampstead: Old-school posh and nouveaux-rich rub shoulders on London's most civilised hilltop. Operates its own version of the Congestion Charge: only vehicles with four-character registration plates are allowed free entry to 'the village'. The tube station's showing its age, but it's only used by the tourists, so who cares?

Hampstead Heath: The verdant jewel in London's crown. Meadows, woods, stately homes, stately views, Bill Oddie, cruising grounds. *See also p150.*

West Hampstead borders: Kilburn, or Cricklewood, depending which estate agent is talking at you.

South Hampstead: A mysterious warren of a billion red-brick mansion blocks and Queen Anne-style turret corners. A simple grid pattern on paper turns into a compass-spinning riddle in practice.

West Hampstead: Impressive-sounding, but mostly a clutter of ageing Victorian housing stock. Why so popular, then? A bevy of good restaurants and the selfish hoarding of all the capital's useful transport links make 'Whampstead' an expensive but convenient neighbourhood. Could do with some decent pubs, mind.

Hampstead Garden Suburb: More celebs, more terracotta, more exclusive and less visited annexe to Hampstead. You have no need to go there.

Hemel Hempstead: Nowhere near Hampstead. Not even in London.

EVER HEARD OF THE COLNEY HATCH FIRE?

Thought not. Some disasters stay with us for ever, and are regularly commemorated. Others seem to fade away, until they rarely surface outside the realms of the obscure quiz question. Of the latter category, one such incident occurred at the 'Colney Hatch Lunatic Asylum' (Friern Barnet) in 1903.

In Edwardian England, if you showed any signs of mental unusualness – depression, say, or even epilepsy – there was a fair chance you'd be labelled a lunatic. So many Londoners were thus branded, that the Colney Hatch hospital was overflowing. Temporary wooden wards had been constructed in the grounds to house the burgeoning patient population. When fire broke out, overcrowding and understaffing led to the deaths of 51 women, making it one of the biggest peacetime tragedies in twentieth-century England. Yet only 100 years on, the UK's worst hospital disaster is all but forgotten. It doesn't even get a mention in the all-seeing Wikipedia, and rarely anywhere else. And that's a tragedy in itself. Colney Hatch, renamed as the Friern Hospital, eventually closed in 1993. It has now been converted into luxury flats.

THE HAMPSTEAD HEATH PONDS
(AND WHAT THEY'RE GOOD FOR)

1. **Men's bathing pond** (cruising of the non-P&O persuasion)

2. **Ladies' bathing pond** (chapel hat pegs)

3. **Mixed bathing pond** (after-party drunken skinny-dipping. Summer only)

4. **'No. 1 Pond'** (watching dogs blatantly disregard the signs that forbid them from entering. Idiots.)

5. **Model boating pond** (models of boating ponds)

6. **Bird Sanctuary Pond** (where?)

7. **'No. 2 Pond'** (fateful spot where avian flu is destined to cross the species barrier)

8. **Kenwood concert pond** (don't know, only the toffs get to see it)

9. **Viaduct pond** (period dramas)

10. **Vale of Health pond** (misnomers)

TREES OF HAMPSTEAD

With the possible exception of Lord Sauron, everybody likes a good tree. And Hampstead's full of 'em. From the ancient Cane Wood (whence 'Kenwood' is derived) to the 'gibbet elms' where highwaymen once hanged, and the original Gospel Oak, this is the arboreal heart of London.

It's a pity, then, that the area's most interesting tree, perhaps the most astounding in the whole of England, is no more. The Great Hollow Elm of Hampstead once stood close to the junction of Haverstock Hill and Pond Street, though its exact location is uncertain. In the seventeenth century, the tree would have been one of the biggest draws in north London.

From descriptions, it sounds like something from Enid Blyton. A solid wooden door in the trunk led to a spiral staircase. Forty-two steps up was an observation turret that could accommodate up to 20 people. It even formed an occasional schoolroom for 12 very distracted scholars.

Alas, no one knows the fate of the great hollow elm. It was last heard of in around 1715, close to the site of a local pub.

HIDDEN HEATH

Hampstead Heath. Such a sprawling and varied place that only someone with lots of time on their hands, and a good pair of shoes on their feet, can ever truly see it all. And that's where we come in. We've crisscrossed the woods, valleys and heathland at all times of day – and night (we won't be doing that again) – so you don't have to. Time to forget Parliament Hill and Kenwood; check out some of the quirkier slices of heathenalia.

First among them must be the Italian Pergola and Hill Garden over on West Heath. A seemingly abandoned walkway of fairytale colonnades, entwined with wisteria, stretches out into the woodlands, commanding spectacular views of Harrow. You can spend hours here watching the wildlife (including a noisy population of woodpeckers) without seeing another soul. That is, unless you stay until twilight, when the surrounding woods seem to become very popular with furtive young gentlemen. No doubt, they come here to coax out badgers.

If, on the other hand, you're looking for a large cock, try Golders Hill park, to the west. Here are all manner of exotic fowl, along with wallabies and small deer.

Crossing back to the main part of the Heath, another good spot to look for wildlife is the north-east tip. These little-visited meadows are perfect for bird and butterfly spotting. And a colony of wild parakeets can often be seen (and certainly heard) swooping between trees. These birds are now common to many of London's parks after allegedly escaping from the studio film-set of *The African Queen* in the 1950s.

Stranger things can be found in the woody parts of the Heath, if you know where to look. In a particularly shady dell, north of the mixed bathing pond, you'll find a number of trees with crucifixes gouged into their barks. Bones and embers often litter the floor around here – perhaps an Ozzy Osbourne hideout. And, elsewhere, ancient boundary markers can be found skulking behind giant oaks, notably near Hampstead Gate.

As with any place of great age, ghost stories abound. Headless highwaymen are said to roam the traditional routes across the Heath, and the Spaniards Inn, to the north-west (*see p153*), is haunted by no fewer than four spectres, including that of highwayman Dick Turpin. Even the bathing ponds are home to tales of phantom footsteps – echoes of the many suicides these pools have attracted.

Finally, fans of ghost tube stations should head over to North End, where the remains of Bull & Bush station can be seen behind the pub of the same name. The platforms and other infrastructure were all completed, yet the station never opened after plans for new housing in the area fell through.

NORTHERN LINE, VICTORIA LINE, FISHING LINE

St John's Wood, someone once discovered, is the only tube station to contain none of the letters of 'mackerel'. But there are some fishy places in north London that can be reached with an Oyster Card:

Tufnell Shark

Codfosters

Harrow-on-the-brill

Tunapike Lane

Tottenham Hake

Finchley Roe

Goldfish Green

Archray

Dolphinsbury Park*

High Barnacle*

(*OK, not fishes, but can you do any better?)

UP CLOSE AND PERSONAL WITH SEVEN SISTERS

If this book is ever digitised, that title alone should draw in the punters. We're talking about a district of London, though, and not some mildly titillating siblings. Seven Sisters lies between Tottenham and Finsbury Park, and is easily reached by the tube. There's little to recommend this place, other than its ancient and mysterious history.

From the station, head east to Broad Lane, and you should find a small green containing seven underwhelming poplar trees (or use Google Earth if you're feeling lazy). These are the seven sisters; not a particularly impressive family, huh?

They were once much grander. The originals were ancient elms, perhaps planted in the fourteenth century by, reputedly, seven sisters who were soon to part. But the site is thought to be ancient; possibly a druidic shrine whose pagan origins are corrupted to the modern name Page Green.

In 1886 the historic elms were withering, and finally cut down. Only one family in the area contained seven sisters, and the Hibbert damsels were drafted in to plant a new circle of elms. This was short-lived, and a further planting was required in 1955, by the Basten sisters. It's these poplars we see today.

Let's hope the trees don't decay once more. A family containing seven sisters is hard to come by these days.

> A large collection of roads and passages which don't go in straight lines, houses of different ages, many of them good architecture but more often it's just the way they fit together, full of nice vistas and surprises. Hampstead is a huge collection of twists and turns.
>
> Mark Pevsner, grandson of architectural historian
> Nikolaus Pevsner, on Hampstead

CROCKER'S FOLLY

Not so far from the Edgware Road, between Little Venice and Lisson Grove, sits the elegantly wasted Crocker's Folly. This huge Queen-Anne-style railway inn lies empty and forgotten some distance from any railway.

The whole sorry legend began when the wealthy Frank Crocker heard, presumably from some bloke down the pub, that a major new rail terminus was to be built across the road. The silly sod didn't bother to check his facts, and hastily went about constructing the sumptuous inn to cash in on the expected train-loads of custom.

But it never came. The terminus was built a fair walk away at Marylebone. Crocker was devastated and some say he hanged himself in his own folly. So the story goes. And who are we to spoil a good yarn in favour of fact? The pub did go on to be a great success but has suffered a downturn in recent years. It's now empty, its future uncertain.

ARCHWAY: SO GOOD THEY NAMED IT TWICE

Archway, along with Crystal Palace and London Bridge, belongs to that exclusive club of Areas Named After Large Structures of Excellence (though the acronym's a bit of a bugger). The structure, here, is a large iron span that carries Hornsey Lane over the A1.

Actually, that might not be true. The area is also said to take its name from a tunnel. Back in the early 1800s, a new northerly traffic route was needed to bypass Highgate Hill (the locals didn't all drive around in 4x4s back then). An arched tunnel, to be called Archway Road, was dug through the ridge beneath Hornsey Road. They got about 320ft in when the whole thing collapsed, forcing a change of plan. Instead, a whole section of ridge was excavated and a John Nash viaduct was built across to carry Hornsey Lane. This has since been replaced by the iron bridge we see today.

The bridge is worth visiting for the champion view of the city, nicely framed by ornate lampposts (like those that line the Thames) and the spiky anti-suicide bars that all too often fail in their task (Archway is also known as Suicide Bridge).

THE SPANIARDS BOTTLENECK

It might be miles from anywhere, but the Spaniards Inn is one of London's top boozers. Not only does it have a full range of fine ales and spirits, you'll also find one of the capital's greatest beer gardens and the heartiest of Sunday roasts.

In fact, you'd be hard challenged to find a guidebook that doesn't list this place prominently. But there's one peculiar feature of the Spaniards that usually goes uncommented on: its habit of frustrating the motorist.

The building comes in two halves: there's the famous pub, and there's the infamous toll house across the road. Infamous because it encroaches upon the highway, squeezing Spaniards Road, like the neck of an egg timer, into one lane. Inevitably, this causes lengthy tailbacks and the occasional 'Spanish omelette' when cars collide.

Both the toll house and the pub have achieved Grade II listed status. Hey presto, neither one can be knocked down or moved, leading to a charming obstruction that even pedestrians struggle to negotiate.

Perhaps traffic lights might ease the problem, but that'd spoil all the fun.

THE EAST END
AND BEYOND

THE EAST END AND BEYOND

DRIVER, FOLLOW THAT WORD!

The etymology of the word 'hackney' is a long and quite confusing one; even the Oxford English Dictionary states that the term has 'engaged the most eminent etymologists'. So strap yourself in and we'll try to track the bugger down through the narrow, winding streets of history.

We'll start at the most obvious place: Old English. Here Hackney would have been known as Hacan leg or 'Hook Island'. So far so simple. But now factor in the fact that the area used to be all fields and was a perfect place to raise horses before flogging them at the nearby Smithfield horse market, and things start getting murky. Why? Because in French 'haquenée' means 'an ambling horse' or a horse specifically bred for its stamina.

And do you know what those horses were used for? You guessed it: pulling carriages, the very same carriages which would later become widely known as 'hackney carriages'.

Yes, now we're lost and, what's more, the meter is running. We'll have to keep going though, because these horses did a lot of work and as a result became pretty dishevelled. And so 'hackney' came to mean 'broken old nag' and anyone hired to do a crappy routine job. Oh, and a prostitute. Then came the 'hackney writers', which was later shortened to just 'hack' which in turn led to the term 'hacker'.

Which brings us to our destination of Bang Up To Date. That'll be fifty quid please mate.

WASTE NOT, **WANT NOT**

A selection from the Menu at St John restaurant, Smithfield,
where the motto is 'Nose to tail eating'.

Dried Salted Pig's Liver, Radishes & Boiled Egg

Roast Bone Marrow & Parsley Salad • Bath Chap & Watercress

Deep Fried Tripe • Chitterlings & Beetroot • Snail, Sausage & Chickpea

Lamb's Tongues & Butterbeans • Crispy Pig's Cheek & Dandelion

---

> **Hackney isn't in the East End – that's the mark of the outsider,
> when you hear someone call Hackney the East End. The East End starts
> two miles down the road, across the border of Bethnal Green.**
> Alexander Baron, *The Low Life*

OOOOOOH MATRON!

The Royal London Hospital is a pretty scary place at the best of times. In the basement is a museum that contains some rather nasty-looking vintage surgical instruments, a selection of Jack the Ripper memorabilia, and original documents detailing both the Crippen and the Christie murders.

Oh, and not forgetting the fact that the Elephant Man used to live there.

In fact, you could argue that having a resident ghost is a bit like overkill. But then, who's going to argue with a ghost?

The 'Lady in Grey' (not be confused with Chris de Burgh's 'Lady in Red') is a Victorian nurse who is said to wander one of the hospital's terminal wards, offering comfort to the patients therein. A nice story you might think... except that it is also told that any poor soul who is visited by the compassionate spectre will be dead by morning.

The real creepiness lies in the details however. Sighters of the Lady in Grey have noted that the apparition cuts off below the knees, a peculiarity that was explained when research revealed that the floor of the terminal ward had been raised by two feet during a restoration.

≡DEATH FACTORY OF E8

In the late 1970s, the east London borough of Hackney became the unlikely capital of the hardcore industrial music scene, when the band Throbbing Gristle moved in.

Named after Yorkshire slang for the erect penis, TG were the country's main exponents of a musical genre that had grown out of disturbing performance art 'happenings' and a complete negation of musical traditions.

Throbbing Gristle's studio was located at 10 Martello Street, right next to London Fields. This proximity to what had been a plague burial site helped the band to decide on a suitable name for their creative HQ: the Death Factory. The building still stands today and is used as artists' studios.

Just five minutes away is Beck Road, where Throbbing Gristle lived and whiled away the hours experimenting with various nasty sonic effects. At one point, after the band became immersed in survivalist literature, they decided to convert the house into a makeshift fortress complete with an alarm system, barbed wire and blacked-out windows. Indeed, if you walk past 50 Beck Road today you'll find the front door painted black and studded with bolts in the shape of a 'psychic cross'. We're betting the current residents don't get bothered by too many salesmen.

A typical TG story from this time concerns the arrival of a band of 'travellers' on waste ground near to the Beck Road house. TG decided that these new neighbours were an unwanted distraction and decided to evict them in the only way they knew how: by beaming 'infrasonic frequencies' into their camp. After suffering disrupted sleep, terrible headaches and unsettling nightmares the travellers dispersed, convinced the area was cursed.

THE INCREDIBLE ROLL-CALL OF TALENT BORN IN LEYTONSTONE

Alfred Hitchcock	Steve Harris (of Iron Maiden)
Derek Jacobi	Fanny Craddock
Damon Albarn	John Drinkwater
David Beckham	Talvin Singh
Graham Gooch	Meera Syal

LIMEHOUSE AND CRIME

'The yellow peril incarnate in one man', is how the author Sax Rohmer described his archetypal villain Fu Manchu (political correctness and racial tolerance not being quite as high on the agenda in those days as they are now).

Rohmer (real name: Arthur Ward) was a journalist who wrote comedy sketches in his spare time, when in 1911 he visited Limehouse in order to track down a legendary criminal overlord known only as Mr King. Rohmer never found Mr King, but he did emerge from the maze of opium dens with the idea for Dr Fu Manchu, the now legendary and undoubtedly racist master Chinese criminal.

The Manchu stories played on the fears of the 'yellow terror' that had manifested itself in US policy in the late 1800s, and had spread around the globe by the time Rohmer picked up his pen.

Limehouse made the perfect setting for the evil genius, as the East End's oldest village was building up a large population of 'Lascars' – the catch-all term for the Asian seamen who, having worked a passage to London, were often paid off as soon as they hit port.

THE DLR

The Docklands Light Railway (DLR) started off life in the early 1980s as a modest little thing designed to connect the City to the redeveloped area around the Isle of Dogs.

But, just as model rail enthusiasts start off with a simple circular track and then don't stop until they've filled half the house and their wives leave them, so the DLR grew and grew until it became the huge, 20 mile network it is today.

Bank, Lewisham, Stratford and, of course, Canary Wharf all rely on this tram-train hybrid, which isn't an official part of the London Underground system since it has separate tracks and rolling stock. Indeed, up until the Bank extension was opened in 1991 the DLR did not venture underground, and when it did the original rolling stock had to be sold off because they weren't suitable for subterranean life (the original carriages were sold to Germany and can now be seen in action on underground line U11 in Stuttgart).

But the best thing about the DLR? The fact that it has no drivers of course. The DLR is completely computer-controlled, so this allows passengers to occupy seats at the very front of the train where they can either a) pretend to be the driver, or b) pretend they're on a rollercoaster. Not that you'd ever be that childish of course.

THE LOWER LEA VALLEY:
FROM GRIME TO GONDOLAS

In 2012 the Olympics will come to the East End of London. A vast sporting metropolis will rise up on the site of the 1,000 acre expanse of industrial land and overgrown waterways that is the Lower Lea Valley, and when that happens it will be difficult to remember just what exactly this grey hinterland once contained.

It's doubtful that anyone will miss the plant on Pudding Mill Lane that recycles cooking fat, or the nearby kebab meat factory (do the two share resources? We sincerely hope not). But, bizarre as it may seem, some locals did hold a special place in their hearts for the Hackney fridge mountain, a gigantic structure of unwanted white goods that held the dubious title of being the largest pile of discarded refrigerators in Europe.

The fridge mountain has gone now, probably to the Home for Unwanted Fridges, but the old Bryant & May Factory building still remains – though it now houses a luxury apartment complex.

The factory was the site of the famous Match Girl's strike of 1888, a key event in the suffragette movement which eventually led to the formation of the first British trade union for women. Now it's a gated community called the Bow Quarter whose only real claim to fame is that it contains the flat of Danny Wallace, recently converted into a 'micronation' called 'Lovely' for a BBC2 television series.

Just down the road is another industrial landmark. On Wallis Road stands the building where the British Xylonite Company manufactured something called Parkesine, the first ever plastic. Today you can find a little plaque announcing this fact, placed a little too high on a brick wall for anyone to notice it.

As for the forgotten canals that wind their way through the area, they are to be turned into the 'Venice of the East End'. The River Lea, which once formed a drainage system for the waste materials pumped out by Victorian chemical plants and rubber factories, will become 'Water City', a £3 billion redevelopment project designed to create a 'lasting legacy' of the 2012 games.

N.B. For a remarkable and loving tribute to the Lower lea Valley, try to track down a copy of St Etienne's film *What Have You Done Today, Mervyn Day?*

Palendri: I love London – it's so wonderfully dirty. And The Beatles – I adore The Beatles. You know The Beatles?

Reggie Kray: No.

Ronald Kray: I believe they know us.

Dialogue from *The Krays* (1990)

PARTS OF THE EAST END YOU'VE PROBABLY NEVER HEARD OF (AND REASONS TO VISIT)

Globe Town (Meath Gardens, the final resting place of Bripumyarrimin, an Australian aborigine cricketer who died of tuberculosis in 1868)

Old Ford (the expansive Victoria Park, which contains remnants of the old London Bridge)

Wallend (watch 1995/96 South Essex Sunday League Division 1 runners up, Wallend Wanderers, as they cause havoc in Silvertown Athletic's penalty area)

Plashet (find out just why it's an anagram of 'the slap')

Cranbrook (pass)

Maryland (it's like going to the States, but with a more disappointing cookie to litter ratio)

Cann Hall (for fans of desolate open spaces, this is close to Wanstead Flats)

Seven Kings (buy a house there. Crossrail is due to stop here, so prices will rocket)

Rippleside (revel in the odour of the UK's largest sewage treatment works, just across the creek)

Goodmayes (relive the top craze of 2004, with some good old-fashioned chav-spotting)

THE FAMOUS BAGEL SHOPS OF BRICK LANE

Brick Lane is of course famous for its curries. And there are a lot of curry houses there, and some of them serve a very nice korma. It's just that the area has recently become a victim of its own success; and as for the touts that the restaurants employ to make sure you eat in their establishment AND NOT ANYONE ELSE'S GODDAMIT, well they're just annoying.

So if you want to avoid all that, but you still want to sample some of the best cuisine Brick Lane has to offer, then you should think about visiting Beigel Bake.

A genuine East End institution, Beigel Bake is a 24-hour bakery that churns out around 7,000 bagels a night. And that's on top of operating as a kind of social centre for the local communty and after-hours hang-out for the hipster kids stumbling out of the nearby bars.

And it's cheaper than a curry: a Beigel Bake bagel costs about 12p the last time we checked. And if you want some salt beef or cream cheese and salmon in there it will set you back a whopping £1.50. London isn't this cheap and this good that often, so don't miss out.

The first character to appear in *EastEnders* (BBC1) seemed to be dead on arrival, although he might just have been playing possum to escape the predatory attentions of his neighbours. In the first two episodes, they have spent their time either abusing each other, fighting in the local pub or, if they are lucky, suffering the last stages of alcoholism. It may well result in a Cockney version of the Jonestown Massacre, and it is hardly a good advertisement for the lovable London spirit: by comparison, *Coronation Street* looks more like Vegetarian Kitchen.

Peter Ackroyd reviews the first two episodes
of *EastEnders* in *The Times* (22 February 1985)

ALFRED HITCHCOCK PRESENTS... **LEYTONSTONE**

Alfred Hitchcock was born at 517 High Road, Leytonstone, the son of a greengrocer. He went on of course to be not only one of the greatest film directors of the twentieth century, but also the most recognisable cameo player within his own work. No surprise then that more than 100 years after he was born the man managed to make another set of cameo appearances, this time on the Underground. In 1999 17 mosaics were commissioned for Leytonstone tube station. Some 80,000 tiles were used to re-create memorable scenes from some of his most famous movies. Not only does Hitchcock pop up in some of them, but so do local landmarks, ensuring that the resulting mosaics have a familiar, yet eccentric air about them.

In the scene from *Rebecca*, the second Mrs de Wintern is loomed over by Mrs Danvers, while behind them in the distance is the local St John's Church

(despite the film being set in Cornwall). *The Rear Window* scene shows James Stewart and Grace Kelly spying on the Green Man pub on the nearby High Road, and the background to *Saboteur* also shows a local street.

Suspicion shows Cary Grant carrying a perhaps poisoned glass of milk, and he pops up again on a rooftop in *To Catch a Thief*, only to be chased by a crop sprayer in *North by Northwest*.

The Wrong Man shows Henry Fonda with Hitchcock reading a newspaper behind him, while elsewhere Hitch reclines with Marlene Dietrich. He is also portrayed as a young boy on the back of a horse outside his father's shop.

Particularly striking are *The Birds* and *Vertigo* tributes; but perhaps the oddest image is a red-faced Hitchcock seemingly sharing a shower with Janet Leigh in *Psycho* while a bemused Anthony Perkins peers in from behind the curtain.

THE SIEGE OF SIDNEY STREET

The story of the siege of Sidney Street is often overlooked in the annals of East End crime, what with Jack the Ripper and the Krays hogging all the limelight. Which is a shame, because there aren't all that many stories that begin with a gang of Latvian anarchists robbing a jewellery shop.

The Latvians in question were led by Peter Piatkow (aka Peter the Painter) and had already been involved in the so-called 'Tottenham Outrage' when in late 1910 they conspired to rob a jewellery shop in Houndsditch.

Unfortunately for the Latvians on the night of the robbery a local man called the police after he heard a tapping noise, which turned out to be the gang tunnelling their way towards their swag. When the unarmed constables arrived the Latvians opened fire, killing three of them. A manhunt was launched and a number of the gang were captured but a good number escaped, including Peter the Painter.

Two weeks later, in the early days of January 1911, an informant who may or may not have been the gang's former landlord entered Arbor Square Police Station and told the constabulary that three of the gang, including Piatkow, were hiding out at 100 Sidney Street.

Some 200 policemen rushed to surround the house and by dawn another gun battle had commenced. Home Secretary Winston Churchill rushed out of his morning bath to attend the scene – indeed there is a famous photograph of Churchill in top hat and fur-collared overcoat, peering round the corner of Sidney Street to glimpse a bit of the action. Churchill's solution to the stand-off was to call for members of the Scots Guard battalion from the Tower of London, who arrived in full battle regalia and proceeded to riddle the house with bullets. It was reported at the time that, despite the chaos, a local postman continued to make his round just a few houses away.

After six hours of stalemate a solution to the siege presented itself when the top floor of the house caught fire. The police gathered outside the house, waiting for the inevitable escape attempt. But suddenly the roof collapsed and the upper floors fell in, burying everyone inside.

Two charred bodies were recovered from the rubble and were identified as Fritz Svaas and Joseph Marx. The body of Peter Piatkow, however, was never found. He had vanished without a trace and his position as an East End anti-hero was confirmed, although to this day historians still debate whether Peter the Painter ever really existed.

> We didn't have nowhere to live, we didn't have nowhere to go
> Till someone said, 'I know this place off Burdett Road.'
> It was on the fifteenth floor, it had a board across the door.
> It took an hour to pry it off and get inside. It smelt as if someone had died.
>
> 'Mile End', Pulp

ALL IN
ON THE CLERKENWELL ROAD

If you were going to look anywhere in London for a little bit of the Las Vegas spirit then the Clerkenwell Road probably wouldn't be at the top of your list (it probably wouldn't even make the middle of the list).

But surprisingly, this lengthy bit of asphalt that helps to connect the West End to the East End also contains one of the busiest poker clubs in Europe: the Gutshot.

Don't be put off by the slightly sinister name, it has nothing to do with the area's gangster-related history and actually relates to a bit of poker terminology concerning an unmade straight. The interior of the club might not be what you expect either. Far from being a smoke-filled den populated by unscrupulous characters and trophy women, the Gutshot serves as a meeting place for people of every age (above 18 anyway), creed and colour from across the capital, all of whom share one thing in common: they like a bit of a gamble.

OK, so it's not quite Vegas, but for the cost of cab ride up to the Clerkenwell Road it's the closest you're going to get, and the food's not bad either.

COCKNEY. A nick name given to the citizens of London, or persons born within the sound of Bow bell, derived from the following story: *A citizen of London being in the country, and hearing a horse neigh, exclaimed, Lord! how that horse laughs! A by-stander telling him that noise was called neighing, the next morning, when the cock crowed, the citizen to shew he had not forgot what was told him, cried out, 'Do you not hear how the cock neighs?'*

A rather fanciful 1811 explanation for the origin of the word 'cockney'. The term has been in use since the thirteenth century, if not earlier. Chambers dictionary suggests that it might derive from the Middle English 'coken-ey', meaning a cock's egg or oddity, or from *coquin*, the French for 'rogue', or from *coquus*, meaning 'cook' in Latin. All of which leaves us none the bleedin' wiser.

GOING LIKE THE CLAPPERS

If you've ever found yourself wondering where exactly the most famous bell foundry in the world resides, then you have purchased the right book. Well done you!

As well as being pretty well-known the Whitechapel Bell Foundry on Whitechapel Road is also very, very old, having been in business since 1570. This makes it Britain's oldest surviving manufacturing company (it must be true, it says so in the *Guinness Book of Records*).

And just when you thought you knew all the exciting stuff there was to know about the Whitechapel Bell Foundry, along comes this revelation:

not only did they make the famous Liberty Bell of Philadelphia here, they were also the people behind the mega-famous Big 'it's the bell not the tower actually' Ben.

On the face of it, this may seem like a particularly impressive CV; after all, they've pretty much got the whole 'famous bell' thing sewn up. However, the next time you're shopping around for someone to make a sodding great dinger you should probably bear in mind that both Big Ben and the Liberty bell are also famous for having cracked.

Maybe someone should ask for their money back.

THE FREEDOM PRESS

As well as being home to the world's oldest bell foundry (*see facing page*) Whitechapel also contains the world's oldest anarchist publishing house (although it's probably a safe bet that the two don't go down the pub together or anything like that).

The Freedom Press on Whitechapel High Street was founded in 1886 and is still going strong to this day, despite the premises being firebombed by the neo-fascist group Combat 18 in 1993 (the front of the building still bears the mark of the attack). The group produces a fortnightly newspaper (unfailingly regular – strange, for a bunch of anarchists), also called *Freedom*, which contains UK and international news and, believe it or not, a quiz. No recipes though.

The building is also home to Britain's largest anarchist bookshop, containing such giggle-a-minute tomes as *The State is Your Enemy*, *Why Work?*, and *Love, Sex and Power in Later Life*.

HOME FOR LOST DOGS

History records a number of land masses that used to surround the Isle of Dogs, but which are now lost due to... erm, rising sea levels.

Peninsula of Poodles · Islet of Irish Setters · Archipelago of Afghans
Atoll of Airedale Terriers · Cape of Cocker Spaniel · Red Setter Ridge
Headland of Hanover Hounds · Pekinese Point

SHOREDITCH BUS STOP FUN

If you ever have occasion to pass through Shoreditch or Old Street on a bus, make sure you sit on the top deck. The locals, being of an artistic bent, are fond of adorning the roofs of their bus shelters with all manner of paraphernalia, from incongruous displays of food to exquisitely presented dog turds.

Early in 2006, a new breed of guerrilla art began to appear on this most unlikely of all canvases. Take one medium sized potato, spray it a gaudy hue, impregnate with cocktail sticks and lob atop a bus shelter of your choice. Hey presto, the latest word in surreal street art. But is it art, or just some talentless local with too much time, and too many vegetables, on his or her hands? Well, go and judge for yourself. Best views are to be had from the upper deck of the 55 or 243, which pass through the heart of Shoreditch.

SOUTH OF
THE RIVER

SOUTH
OF THE RIVER

THE BRIXTON WINDMILL

If you ever get into an argument with some pub bore who insists on reaffirming the superiority of north London over the south, there's one sure-fire way of shutting them up, and it goes something like this: 'Ah... yeah... but... there's no windmill in north London, is there?'

Built in 1816, the 39-foot-tall Brixton Mill sits in the rather obviously titled Windmill Gardens in Brixton Hill, and is the only surviving example of a dozen or so windmills that used to operate in Lambeth. The mill was still being used up until the 1920s, although the term 'windmill' became a bit of a misnomer around the early twentieth century when surrounding buildings got in the way of the wind and other means (such as steam and gas) had to be employed to shift the sails.

The windmill is a listed building and is under the guardianship of Lambeth Council, but is falling into disrepair. It is currently boarded up and closed to the public, but it is possible to visit it on London's annual 'Open House' weekend.

A FEW MODERN ALTERNATIVES TO 'THE MAN ON THE CLAPHAM OMNIBUS'

The hoody on the stolen scooter

The mariachi band on the Northern line

The yummy mummy in the Chelsea tractor

The Tory backbencher on Clapham Common

The Doherty on the smack

The tourist on the wrong side of the escalator

The happy slapper on the ASBO

VAUXHALL AND SPY

If you cross over the Thames using Vauxhall Bridge you can't help but notice the premises at 85 Vauxhall Cross looming up at you from the left. Surprisingly, this unmistakable and distinctive building is home to one of the most covert organisations in the world: the Secret Intelligence Service, or MI6.

Built in the late 1980s to house Britain's foreign intelligence gatherers, the building cost around £150 million to construct. There are rumours that a tunnel links the building to Whitehall, and it is said that the glass in the windows is 3.5in thick. It's also really, really ugly.

However, the building's aesthetics probably weren't behind the rocket attack that occurred in September 2000. No one claimed responsibility after a Russian-built Mark 22 anti-tank weapon was used to fire a missile at the eighth floor, causing slight damage to the wall, but the general consensus was that the Real IRA were behind it.

Arguably a far more dangerous breach of the nation's security occurred in March of the same year when an MI6 spook left his laptop in a taxi, apparently after downing one too many in the nearby tapas bar Rebatos (you should visit, their patatas bravas is to die for).

MI6 top brass quickly swung into action... by taking out an ad in the *Evening Standard* offering a substantial reward for the recovery of a PhD student's 'vital research notes'. The computer was recovered by the Met a week later.

85 Vauxhall Cross is also a bit of a film star, having appeared in no less than three James Bond films. Its finest moment probably came at the beginning of *The World Is Not Enough*, when Pierce Brosnan exits the building in a speedboat in order to chase a bad guy down the Thames.

BIG TROUBLE
IN LITTLE BALHAM

Mention 'the Priory' to anyone in south London today and they'll probably think you're talking about the showbiz community's rehab centre of choice over in Leatherhead. But in the late nineteenth century mention of the Priory would have led directly to thoughts of Balham and murder, sex and intrigue.

In 1876 the Priory was the grandest house in Balham, owned by a Mr Charles Bravo right up until the point when he was killed there by a dash of poison slipped into his bedside drink; this is reported to have been laudanum, well known at the time to be a cure for toothache.

The coroner's inquest (which took place in the building that today houses the Bedford Arms pub) brought to light a series of revelations that captivated the nation. They didn't have *Heat* magazine in those days remember.

However these tales of extramarital affairs, abortion, disgruntled maids and inherited fortunes only served to muddy the waters and the case was never solved.

Since then many amateur sleuths have taken on the task of trying to solve the case; the latest theory suggests that it was Bravo's wife wot dunnit because her husband was after a bit of nooky. A theory the men of Balham should maybe bear in mind the next time their wives complain of 'a headache'.

HAIR TODAY...
PUNTASTIC HAIRDRESSERS FROM SOUTH OF THE RIVER

Hairloom (Fulham, SW6)

Cutting Room (Streatham High Rd, SW16)

Hairport (Southwark, SE16)

Upper Cuts (Nunhead Green, SE15)

Hairetage Hairdressing (Lavender Hill, SW11)

Head South (Northcote Rd, SW11)

Shear Class (Peckham, SE15)

Beyond the Fringe (Woolwich, SE18)

Up 'N Cutting (Eltham, SE9)

"

You know it means no mercy
They caught him with a gun
No need for the Black Maria
Goodbye to the Brixton sun
You can crush us
You can bruise us
But you'll have to answer to
Oh – the guns of Brixton.

'The Guns of Brixton',
The Clash (Paul Simonon)

"

SOUTH LONDON'S SHAMEFUL ROAD

In 2002 Streatham High Road was awarded the extremely dubious honour of being Britain's worst street, in a poll organised by the BBC and the Commission for Architecture and the Built Environment (CABE).

Listeners to BBC Radio 4's 'Today' programme dubbed the High Road Britain's number one 'Street of Shame' and CABE called it 'depressing', mainly because of the area's urban decay and chaos-enducing traffic congestion. One 'single ever-shifting traffic cone' was rather unfairly singled out as a prime offender.

Strangely enough, Streatham High Road is also a conservation area, designated as being 'of special architectural or historic interest' by Lambeth Council.

This rather contradictory state of affairs has resulted in a £200,000 project to try to improve the appearance of the road and its shopfronts. The first initiatives included getting rid of all the (overflowing) rubbish bins, and hanging banners from lampposts declaring how great the area is.

Shoot the Aged: A non-charitable profit making organisation using non-voluntary staff

Name and signage on a pine furniture shop in Lee, south London. Now, sadly, closed down.

THE **DRUG-CRAZED** SQUIRRELS OF BRIXTON

In October of 2005 the local south London press ran stories claiming that the recent anti-drug strategies in Brixton town centre had caused crack cocaine dealers to abandon their usual stash hideouts and start concealing crack rocks in people's front lawns.

The result: crack squirrels!

Local residents reported seeing squirrels frantically digging in their flower-beds, a rather hungry look in their bloodshot eyes. Scotland Yard denied all knowledge of the phenomenon, but this only served to fuel the rumours and soon the national press was having a field day.

Urban myths from across the Atlantic told of addict squirrels in the parks of New York and Washington, DC attacking locals in their search for a fix, and soon rumours began to circulate that London may soon be held hostage by drug-crazed bushy-tailed gangs armed with sharpened pine cones.

To date this nightmare scenario has yet to materialise, but if you're in the Brixton area and are approached by a squirrel trying to sell you a car stereo then it's probably best to keep walking.

A SELECTION OF BOAT RACE FACTLETS

- The early Boat Races took place at Westminster, but when this got too crowded the race was moved six miles up-stream to Putney.

- In 1877 the race was declared a dead heat because, rumour has it, the judge was asleep under a bush and missed the finish.

- In 2003 Oxford won by less than a foot.

- In case of an emergency, each team has two extra rowers called 'the spare pair'.

- Boats have sunk on four occasions: Oxford got their feet wet once in 1925, while Cambridge have gone for a paddle twice (1859 and 1978). In 1912 the race had to be rescheduled when both boats sank.

- 1987 saw the infamous Oxford mutiny when a number of American oarsmen refused to row after a fellow Yank was replaced by the English President (and fantastically named) Donald Macdonald. Oxford went on to win regardless.

- In 1999 Cambridge included Josh West in their team. At 6ft 9in he is the tallest man in Boat Race history.

- Olympic gold medallist Matthew Pinsent has rowed for Oxford three times.

- Other famous boat race rowers down the years include Hugh Laurie and Lord Snowdon (both Cambridge boys).

- Boat race is cockney rhyming slang for 'face'.

UP THE MISSING JUNCTIONS

Visitors to London lucky enough to fly to gentlemanly Gatwick Airport but stupid enough to decide to journey into town by road will find themselves travelling in on the M23. Joining the motorway at Junction 9, they'll soon wonder why, merely two junctions later, they're forced off and dumped onto the motorway's A road namesake. Slowly and painfully wending their way through the less-than-picturesque London Borough of Croydon, weary travellers will have plenty of time to ponder the stupidity of a motorway that terminates at Junction 7 and wonder what happened to junctions 1 to 6.

Abandoned in 1979, the M23 was originally intended to stretch all the way into Streatham, a good 11 or so miles further into London. The plan was to join the M23 to the South Circular, as a solution to the rising levels of London traffic. Scuppered by nimbyism and escalating cost estimates, perhaps Londoners should be thankful that it never came to fruition, given the reputation of the M25 as Britain's largest car park.

THE BATTLE
OF BATTERSEA MURAL

In July 1979 a huge crowd came together in Battersea to try to save one of the area's most treasured landmarks: a mural entitled *The Good, The bad and The Ugly*.

Known locally as just 'The Battersea Mural', the painting was designed by the local artist Brian Barnes and painted by a team of volunteers between 1976 and 1978. Stretching for 256ft on the wall of the empty Morgan Crucible Company factory on Battersea Bridge Road, the mural was immediately controversial.

While the 'Good' section celebrated all that was great about the local area and its inhabitants, the other sections depicted Battersea's less impressive elements, such as the disused crucible factory itself, and even a burning Mickey Mouse, included to signify the abortive attempt to build a Disneyland in Battersea Park.

In the summer of 1979 two-thirds of the mural was destroyed when the Morgan Crucible Company sent bulldozers to demolish the old factory to make way for a new office block. After a local outcry, questions were asked in Parliament, and a round-the-clock vigil was set up to protect the final section.

On 7 July the protest came to a head and police arrested seven demonstrators, including Barnes himself, while the bulldozers forced the crowd away, and the last remnants of the mural were reduced to dust.

Brian Barnes continues to decorate south London; his works include the *Seaside Picture* on Thessaly Road and *Nuclear Dawn* in Brixton. In November 2005 Barnes hit the papers again after he added a picture of Jean Charles de Menezes, the young Brazilian shot and killed at Stockwell underground station by the police, to the Stockwell memorial garden mural without seeking the local council's authorisation.

> **The people have such an attitude. Especially the kids; they all have that 'I'm from south London' thing going on. I have relatives in Clapham – which is OK – but I only go and see them once a month if I can help it.**
> Minicab driver interviewed in *Time Out* magazine (2006, issue 1843)

DESCRIPTIONS OF THE MILLENNIUM DOME
(SEE IF YOU CAN SPOT THE ODD ONE OUT)

- 'a partly flattened mushroom punctured by a circle of 12 pins' – Encyclopedia Britannica

- 'the biggest fridge magnet in the world' – cultural critic AA Gill

- 'a heap of icing sugar with 12 match-ends stuck in it' – writer Iain Sinclair

- 'a monstrous blancmange' – Prince Charles

- 'a pustulated cyst under acupuncture' – Paul Ford of www.Ftrain.com

- 'a very bad hair transplant' – comedian David Baddiel

- 'a sinister abattoir disguised as a circus tent' – writer JG Ballard

- 'a desperate, empty, national grandiosity' – journalist Hugo Young

- 'a creation that, I believe, will truly be a beacon to the world' – The Rt Hon Tony Blair MP, Prime Minister

---

POWER TO THE PEOPLE!
Tooting is probably best known for being the stomping ground of Wolfie Smith, south London's answer to Che Guevara (and a lifelong Fulham supporter).

The 1970s sitcom *Citizen Smith* was the creation of John Sullivan and starred Robert Lindsay as Wolfie Smith, the enthusiastic and self-proclaimed leader of the Tooting Popular Front, a four-strong band of Marxist revolutionaries whose main aim was 'freedom for Tooting'.

Modern Tooting is, unfortunately, still under the rule of the fascist despots of the local council, but it is still possible to make a pilgrimage to the source of the area's most famous fictional resident. Simply hop on a bus to South Wimbledon, where you'll find a pub with the unlikely name of the Nelson Arms. It was here, in 1968, that Sullivan encountered a rather drunken and gobby local man whom he later described as 'a Master Dreamer in an age of fantasy' and on whom he based the character of Wolfie Smith.

Sullivan of course then went on to do even more damage to south London's reputation, by writing the Peckham-based *Only Fools and Horses*.

STARSPOTTING IN THE SOUTH

Forget The Ivy and Nobu, when it comes to celeb stalking south of the river is where it's at.

Circle Bar, Clapham Road, SW9. When Mike 'The Streets' Skinner has finished drying his eyes this is where he comes to wet his whistle.

Mayfair Snooker Club, Tooting High Street, SW17. Jimmy 'not as whirlwind as he used to be' White has been known to frequent this club, and sometimes he even plays a bit of snooker.

Geraldine Mary Harmsworth Park, Southwark, SE1. Kevin Spacey rather famously likes to take his dog for a walk here in the early hours of the morning. If you see him, don't ask to borrow his phone as he's likely to get upset.

Brixton, SW9. Remember Carter the Unstoppable Sex Machine? No? Well anyway 'Fruitbat' (not his real name) is a lifelong resident of Brixton and can often be seen perusing the local market.

Hot Stuff Curry House, Wilcox Road, SW8. Writer and broadcaster Will Self once took heroin on John Major's plane, but when he fancies a Korma this is where he comes.

Stealth House, Camberwell, SE5. Comedian Jenny Éclair lives here in her rather striking award-winning, black and white 'Californian beach house'.

SO.UK, Clapham High Street, SW4. This Moroccan/Asian Pacific bar and restaurant is brought to you by 'golden couple' Lesley Ash and Lee Chapman.

THE FINE ART OF TOOTHBRUSH HOLESMANSHIP

In the 1950s the renowned comedy writing team of Frank Muir and Dennis Norden penned a sketch designed to lampoon the overly enthusiastic style of the American travelogue.

Vaunting the merits of 'glorious Bal-ham', the sketch celebrates this 'gateway to the south'. It remarks in particular upon the quaint old stores of the high street and its world-famous craftsmen, who indulge in the delicate art of boring holes in the top of toothbrushes, also known as toothbrush holesmanship:

'It is exciting work and my forefathers have been engaged upon it since 1957. The little holes are put in manually or in other words: once a year.'

The skit was made famous by the great Peter Sellers, who played all the Balham-based characters throughout the sketch. More recently it was filmed by none other than former Monkee Mickey Dolenz, who cast a very young Robbie Coltrane in at least 15 of the roles.

THE BEAST OF BEXLEY

Want to see big cats without forking out £13 to get into the zoo? Then head down to the south-east to visit London's accidental safari park. Over the past couple of years, an astonishing number of beastly sightings have occurred in an area centred, at least for alliterative purposes, on Bexley.

Some say it's a puma, others a panther. But evidence is scant. An inconclusive footprint here, a mauled fox carcass there. The only tangible bit of 'proof' is a fuzzy photo taken by a Sidcup housewife in 2006, which appears to show a black, feline form walking through long grass.

So what's going on? Is this an escapee pet, an overgrown tabby, or a stunt by the Bexley tourist board? London's answer to the Loch Ness monster remains an enigma.

ALL YOU EVER WANTED TO KNOW ABOUT

THE WOMBLES OF WIMBLEDON

- Author Elisabeth Beresford came up with the name 'Womble' after one of her children referred to Wimbledon Common as 'Wombledon Common'.

- As well as the famous TV series there was a rather disturbing-sounding live-action movie, starring David Tomlinson, Bonnie Langford and Kenny 'R2-D2' Baker.

- Below a certain age, all Wombles are nameless. How creepy is that?

- The life expectancy of an average Womble is 200+ years.

- During the run of the TV series the press reported that children were attempting to 'bait' Wombles by dropping litter onto Wimbledon Common.

- There was a Womble from the East End called Stepney. He had dreadlocks.

- For one of the Wombles' appearances on *Top of the Pops*, the costumes were filled by members of Steeleye Span.

- The Borrible trilogy of books written by Michael de Larrabeiti feature the Rumbles, a group of giant, intelligent rat-like creatures who are apparently based on the Wombles.

- The only Womble not named after a place is Chairman Womble Wong.

- Beresford once travelled to South Africa where she read her Womble stories to some 1,000 Zulu warriors. They were apparently 'enchanted'.

ACKNOWLEDGEMENTS

Collectively we would like to thank all the Londonist.com contributors past and present; all our loyal readers (even the pedantic ones who point out our mistakes); and the people at Gothamist.com for helping us to keep doing what we enjoy doing most: writing about our city.

Mike: To Mike Brewer, the first real Londoner I ever met – a rich, vibrant and generous person who reflected all that is good about this city. And Jess for her love, support and ability to cope with my watching *An American Werewolf in London* almost continually since we met.

William: To my wife Hazel, looking forward to future explorations of the city, and to my grandmother Prilly, my first and favourite authority on London.

Rob: To my wife Nina, for putting up with the geekiness.

Matt: What Rob says, but Nina = Heather and geekiness = uber-geekiness.

Kenneth: Thanks to Polly and Tiger and Minxy.

FURTHER READING

London the Biography, Peter Ackroyd

The Annals of London, John Richardson

The Buildings of England: London vol 1-6, Nikolaus Pevsner et al

London, England, Derek Hammond

A Traveller's Companion to London, Thomas Wright (ed)

Do Not Pass Go, Tim Moore

Walking Haunted London, Richard Jones

Smoke, A London Peculiar, Matt Haynes, Jude Rogers (eds)

London A Short History, AN Wilson

Hampstead Heath: the Walker's Guide, David McDowall and Deborah Wolton,

Underground London, Stephen Smith

The London Companion, Jo Swinnerton

London Writing, Merlin Coverley

Foyles: A Celebration, Penny Mountain with Christopher Foyle

The London Compendium: A Street-by-street Exploration of the Hidden Metropolis, Ed Glinert (Ed)

One Stop Short Of From Barking, Mecca Ibrahim

Mother London, Michael Moorcock

253, Geoff Ryman

Underground to Everywhere, Stephen Halliday

The Subterranean Railway: How the London Underground Was Built and How It Changed the City Forever, Christian Wolmar

What's in a Name?: Origins of Station Names on the London Underground, Cyril M Harris

www.londonist.com

london-underground.blogspot.com

http://london.thewayweseeit.org

http://rachelnorthlondon.blogspot.com

www.plasticbag.org

http://randomreality.blogware.com

diamondgeezer.blogspot.com

http://onionbagblog.blogspot.com

www.banksy.co.uk

www.classiccafes.co.uk

www.victorianlondon.org

http://londonreviewofbreakfasts.blogspot.com

www.inkycircus.com

We haven't had a good juicy series of sex murders since Christie. And they're so good for the tourist trade. Foreigners somehow expect the squares of London to be fog-wreathed, full of hansom cabs and littered with ripped whores, don't you think?

Alfred Hitchcock, *Frenzy*, 1972

NOTES

OTHER TITLES BY THINK BOOKS

London's Royal Parks
London's Royal Parks is a celebration of some of the capital's – and the UK's – most well-known, best-loved and historically important public spaces. Published in association with The Royal Parks Foundation, it is an essential addition to any contemporary coffee table, combining stunning photography of present-day parks, with eye-opening historical narrative and inspiring anecdotes, poetry and prose.
ISBN 1-84525-014-1, £20

Tales from the Tower
From the luxurious to the lethal, the Tower of London has been subject to a wealth of mishaps, myths and misconceptions for nearly 1,000 years. Originally designed by William the Conqueror just after the Battle of Hastings as the country's greatest fortress, it has since become a palace, a prison, a torture chamber, a place of execution, an armoury, a giant safe, a mint and a menagerie! *Tales from the Tower* contains all the secrets and superstitions from its glorious and gory past.
ISBN 1-84525-026-5, £9.99

The London Companion
From Edgware to Morden, Upminster to Ealing, no stone has been left unturned to bring you this astonishing collection of facts, figures and very tall stories about the incomparable city of London. All the world is here, from prehistoric animals to Viking kings, medieval riots to modern art. Part of the Companion Series by Think Books.
ISBN 1-86105-799-7, £9.99

Hampstead
and the North

Is
Cl

Regent's Park
and Camden Town

Oxford Street, Mayfair, Wes
St James's, Westminster,
Embankment, Trafalgar Sq
Soho, Covent Garden

Hyde Park

Notting Hill
and the West

Chelsea